Between The Streetlights & Red Lights

'Escaping from Human Trafficking,

Sexual Slavery and Exploitation'

By Jack W Gregory

This book is dedicated to the ones that didn't make it and to those still stuck in that life. You are loved and we will do our very best to fight for you and for your memories.

www.warcrypress.co.uk

The Chapters in this book are written and based upon interviews with the survivor concerned. In every interview a plan was made with the survivor on how to set the chapter out. Some of the chapters were basic transcripts of the interviews with only basic changes made to make it more readable. Other chapters have been written to flow more like a chapter and read more like a story. In each case every care was taken to preserve the voice of the survivor and agreed only after the survivor agreed its final form.

There are chapters that were sent to me that only went through proof reading and basic editing and others that were written as letter form by the author and survivor. Every care and consideration has been taken by the author and the publisher to bring the reader an authentic book of survivor stories that honours the survivor.

The book has been written this way to not only preserve the voice of the survivor and also project the voice of the author, however we should point out that due to the context of this book and the way it is structured it does represent a wide range of views that may not necessarily represent the view of the publisher or author.

£1 from this book goes to:

Hope Community Church, Wymondham

Registered Charity Number: 1126428

The Magdalene Group offers a variety of front-line projects, aimed at raising awareness and preventing the sexual exploitation of women and young people.

The Magdalene Group | Registered Charity No: 1041195

Acknowledgements

I would like to thank all of the beautiful and courageous souls who have contributed to the research and testimonies for this book and the chapters therein, giving special thanks to the following:

My Partner Joanna for her love and support, I love you.

My Daughter Regan for her love and support, daddy loves you.

Matty, Jess, Alice and Freddie, my step kids, I may not be your father but I love you all the same.

My Publisher's Warcry Press.

Mr Grantley Watkins for his contribution and friendship

Mrs Rosey Leeder for her help and support

Mr Andy Jones

Ms Jesse Hepburn for her outstanding contribution to this book.

To Rockstarr Ministries Facebook Group

Mr Leighton Porter from Gangland and Prison Related

To Joanna Hogg, for your continuing support and advice.

To John Wilthew, Andy Latham, Mark Bullen and Angela Kemm for your sound advice as always that has helped greatly in writing this book.

About the Author

Long Story Short …

Jack (William) Gregory Is an Actor, Writer, Director, Poet, Photographer, Musician, Producer and Loving Father based in Wymondham, Norfolk, UK. He was born in Glasgow in 1977 and Lovingly Raised by his adoptive parents in Normanton, West Yorkshire.

During his brief 40 years walking the roads of this world He was an accomplished Magician, he trained briefly as an actor in youth with Local and National Theatre groups.

He trained in creative writing at the Yorkshire Arts Circus under Ian Clayton (albeit briefly). He was a performance poet under the mentorship and guidance of Karl Dallas (again albeit briefly) winning several poetry awards.

Jack had lived a troubled life for a long time, he not only fought addiction, he fought to escape from crime and violence for many years.

After a Long spell of illness Jack has yet again begun to rebuild his life. His first ever published work comes in the form of Four commissioned poems about Legendary Heavyweight Boxer and Hard-man Paul Sykes, for Jamie Boyle's Best Selling books Sykes: Unfinished Agony and Further Agony from War Cry Press.

Incidentally Jack knew and occasionally worked alongside Paul as a Debt Collector in his younger days.

Jack is now under the care and guidance of Hope Community Church, Wymondham. He is also training under The School of Supernatural Life Program.

Note from the Author

This book contains honest testimonies from real survivors and escapees of Sexual Slavery and Human Trafficking. Some of the accounts in this book are in depth and speak frankly and in detail about the abuse they have suffered, and although this is not gratuitous, some may find the openness and frankness in the accounts upsetting and disturbing and whilst I have taken the care and time to attempt to minimize the offence, the impact is still there.

Upon writing this book and speaking to the survivors I have made a promise to allow each and every one of them to speak as openly as they wished and agreed to minimize the censorship. I want this book to affect each and every reader in a profound way. Whether this book could be classed as "a good book" is irrelevant. Everyone involved in this book has a singular aim, for it to be so impacting to the reader that they want to do something to help put an end to Human Trafficking and Sexual Slavery. Although every personal account is different, they all share the all too common and heartbreaking truths. We can only hope that this book can help put across the point that trafficking and sexual slavery is wrong and needs to end.

Unfortunately we live in a world where sex and sexuality sells and as difficult as it may sound, so do people. We need to understand that human beings are not for sale, we are not objects, we are not stock for commercial or personal use, we are worth far more than that. We have no price. We are people, not profit.

Contents

Author's Introduction

My first book; A Personal Apocalypse, the poetic ramblings of a troubled man was very much about me. It was a personal need to exorcise some of my own personal demons. After I finished writing the book I was left with a need to write more, but what could I write about? I did not really want to write more about myself at that time and some of the other books I had lined up about other people (mostly crime and boxing) had fallen through. Also, to be honest I am not really in the right frame of mind for fiction at the moment, it's not really my forte if I am being truthful, well that is not strictly true, I do write fiction for the screen and that has taken most of my time in the past so, I wanted something different. Needless to say, I was left with quite the quandary.

Over the past 3 or so years I have been going through quite a change mentally, physically and especially spiritually. My Christian journey had begun to feel a little stale. I struggled to find my way in my faith. I had no idea what God wanted for me and did not yet understand how to listen, so I enrolled in the School of Supernatural course at my church and that is where I began to grow into my own, so I prayed and listened.

I knew that I would dedicate my time to writing but I felt led to giving a platform to those who are unable to communicate effectively, to those who need a voice and then my good friend Ria Landon came to mind. Ria was trapped in Sexual Slavery for many years from childhood. Her own journey led her to write her own international bestselling books with Harper Collins; Daddies Little Earner and Escaping Daddy. Her journey has taken her from sexual slavery that began in childhood to a devout Christian and outspoken campaigner against human trafficking and sexual slavery.

Over time I have been given several words of encouragement from members of my home church, Hope Community Church, Wymondham.

After some prayer and reflection I believe wholeheartedly that this book is what I was mean to do. My whole life has been on the narcissistic side and I have always given myself a voice. I now feel and believe that I am supposed to act as mouthpiece for those who are not able to communicate effectively or are too fearful of using their own voice to speak against

1

injustice. Hence Streetlights and Red Lights was born out of that necessity. All of that being said, please do not think this is a book that is going to speak about religion and force it upon you, it is not. I speak of my faith because it is relevant to the origin of this book. Streetlights and Red lights is a book not only of testimony from the survivors' perspective it offers a real insight into the whole murky world of human trafficking and sexual slavery.

This book has very much become a personal mission and eye opening experience. Every single testimony in this book has affected me in such a profound way both mentally and spiritually. I have shed so many tears whilst transcribing my notes. In my research I have not only learned about the trades of Human Trafficking and Sexual Slavery, I have learned so much about myself and my own behavior and views on women over the years and I have to confess that my intentions towards women have not always been honorable. In the past I have used women for my own sexual gratification, for my own selfish reasons. Writing this has made me question so much of my life and so many decisions I have made in my personal life. Like many men, I have viewed Pornography and Sexualization as normal. I have looked upon women not as women but as objects of desire and realising this, I found the need to change my perception of women and sex.

Within my own personal life, in my younger days I was a victim of abuse from a trusted friend, yet my own journey has led me to treating women the way I did. I am a Fiancée, a father, a brother, a son and I did not realize my own views could very well affect them.

Women should be honored for who they are, for what they do. Strong and powerful. If I could wish this book to do anything it would be to honor them as fighters, as survivors and as the beautiful children of God they are.

Whilst I was researching and looking for contributors to this book I was not only astounded but deeply saddened and heartbroken by some of the attitudes held by many. It was mostly hyper masculine, misogynistic comments by men that should know better. Most I put down to Internet trolling, some I put down to lack of knowledge and a fearful attitude, the latter I have personally been guilty of at times. The things that I have not

2

understood, been embarrassed about (both for myself and them), the attitude I held and my immediate response would be to hide in my own dark humor and make inappropriate comments and jokes to cover up my own shortcomings.

There were however some comments from other females that really touched the bone, that lies beyond bad taste and most of the comments cleared that line with room to spare, hence I cannot and will not repeat. I have realized through this whole process that people really do need to be educated on this matter. We live in a generation where we are desensitized to sex, to violence, to gore. We live in a world that is dominated by YouTube, social media and MEMES that push the boundaries of taste to a whole different level. We see violent videos masked as humor and ever growing sexual content and that is desensitizing us to the reality of sexual objectification and exploitation. Books like this tear open the lies of objectification and are needed more than ever. We need to realize that exploitation will carry on whilst there is a need and unfortunately society judges the need as high and things are getting worse very quickly.

What is Human Trafficking?

"The action or practice of illegally transporting people from one country or area to another, typically for the purpose of forced labour or commercial sexual exploitation".

It is a heartbreaking fact that in 2018 Slavery still exists in the so called free world and the business that turns people into marketable products. The buying, selling and transportation of human beings is very much a business and sadly business is booming. Forced labour, sexual slavery and commercial sexual exploitation is a multi billion pound business both here in the UK and USA although it happens all over the world and the figures are truly, horrifically alarming.

There are several different sides to the trade, these involve:

- Providing a spouse for the purpose of forced marriage
- The removal of organs including ova for the purpose of illegal and unregistered IVF
- Forced and unregistered surrogacy
- Forced commercial manual labour
- Forced commercial sexual slavery

According to **Unseen.org**, in 2016 there were almost 21 million people worldwide who are victims of forced labour.

That is 11.4 million women and girls and 9.5 million men and boys and of those 4.5 million are forced into sexual exploitation. In 2018 this is an estimated 20 to 37 million globally.

The private economy generates 150 billion dollars of illegal profits in the USA alone.

In 2016, in the UK 3,805 potential victims of trafficking were identified and of those 1278 were children.

Victims of the trade are identified as a wide range of men, women and children of all race and ethnicity, although it is usually more prevalent among the more vulnerable in society or socially excluded groups, the trade will make money from anyone and anyone could be a potential victim.

Approximately 51% of victims in the UK are Women and 48% are men (of which 1% are Transsexual).

Limited opportunity at home, poverty, lack of education, unstable and political conditions, economic imbalance and War are listed as key factors that contribute to the slave trade, abuse and exploitation of human beings.

It is highlighted that victims can and often do face more than one form of exploitation.

In 2016 potential victims were identified from 108 countries of origin. The top 7 countries are as follows;

- Albania
- Vietnam
- The United Kingdom
- Nigeria
- China
- Romania
- Poland

18% of all referrals to the National Referral Mechanism in 2015 were from Albania. From 2015 the UK has seen a 17% increase of the number of referred potential victims of trafficking.
Facts and figures from **unseen.org.**

Streetlights and Red lights
© Jack W Gregory 2018

As the night falls
As the light fails
As darkness begins to prevail

There she is

Hidden in plain sight
Inconspicuous, Incognito
Obvious only to those who know

As she stands solemnly between the Pathways and alleyways
There she stands, her face obscured in the shadows of the streetlights and
red lights

And where she stands, she stands alone
Truly alone

For her mind and body travel a separate, dangerous, juxtaposed path

The men
They come in their crawling cars

Trawling the streets looking to exploit her with pictures of the queen
masked as money and it's not worth the paper it is printed on because to
her each note is exactly as it says

"I promise to pay the bearer on demand the sum of X pounds"
It is nothing but a means to an end

To clothe her, to put food on the table, to sustain, to survive
Her body used and abused, her very essence subdued for that promise, that
paper promise

A promise for a good meal, a room for the night
Nothing more, nothing less

And the cars they stop, and the window winds down
And every time she forces a smile to hide the pain of what is about to come

Every time, every touch a little more of her hope fades

"Just a few pounds for my time sir"
"For whatever you like sir"
"Your needs not mine sir"
"Just enough to get by sir"

And those paper promises cloud her mind
Suffocate and leave her soul bereft and breathless
And the men so selfish, thinking of nothing more than their own seedy,
greedy, depraved desires and lustful intent
They want nothing more than to be satisfied, gratified as she is sexualized
and objectified, and they leave her used and abused by the roadside

As she is left more than disheveled, picking up the pieces of her shattered
heart

And the men go home to their lives
To their children and to their wives
To live in the lie of a happy life
The 2.4 children
The token wife
A family life
But he objectifies them just the same

Literally:
© Jesse Hepburn 2018

Snuff films are like porn on crack, you do one and you never get your life back.

Literally

If it takes watching women get murdered for money to turn you on honey then maybe you have more in common with Ted Bundy.

Literally

If you think snuff films are short tobacco ads, good for you, you're still an innocent soul.

Literally

Literally snuff films are videos that snuff out the life of someone's mother, aunt, child or daughter.

But the worst part is while survivors of gun violence protest and march for their lives, and are able to grieve on the national mall and in the public spotlight…..

Those who grieve for the loss of their sister survivors do so in the back halls of seedy motels or in the light of a car dash or a street lamp or a cell phone open to social media.

Literally

Via social media survivors connect fellow sisters to secretly hold vigils and light candles and literally thank and curse God that they still walk this earthly sod, whilst their sisters do not.

Dear Grandfather
© Jesse Hepburn 2018

Dear Grandfather

It's ironic that I can call you Grandfather again. I cannot call you grandpa because I had one of those for real on the other side of the family that is definitely not you, but I can now at last call you Grandfather instead of Kenneth. It may seem like a small thing but it's a giant leap for me personally.

I used to find comfort in the hope you were in hell. Now I am tempted to think you would have fit in really well with Satan and not realized hell in the way I hoped you experienced it, then I just decided one day to worry about where you are spending eternity is a waste of my time and I don't have to think about you or please you or fear you anymore. The floodgates open. So many memories of you and the club of men and women and the other children and the music and especially the pictures and films.

Memories of alcohol and watching people take bad acid trips. Memories of suicide, and death and snuff films. Memories of red light rooms and memories of trading fake names.

Mostly though I remember never wanting to be a "wife" because it was always the wife's fault you and all the other men had to find sexual release with me or had to pay me to fulfill the sex role she would not.

The cool thing though is it feels really good to flip you the bird, pet my two cats who now share my bed and lay here writing this with my hair chopped short and dyed blue and wearing completely mismatched pajamas and pink underwear, and turn the bedroom light off. To do all that and to know I'm safe and I'm okay, I am here and I survive.

Survivor: Jesse Hepburn

There is a strong survivor narrative around being an incest survivor and being more susceptible to human trafficking or being controlled by a pimp. In essence grooming is grooming and once the boundary of sexual abuse is crossed, especially with a child, the distinction between only the perpetrator or many perpetrators becomes moot.

Yet there is very little discussion within the survivor community about how many times the person who trafficked us and was our pimp was also a relative, or became one through marriage to us directly or by marrying our mothers.

I was trafficked by my Grandfather. From my earliest memories of being in a bassinet beside the bed whilst he had sex with my Grandmother. to being a toddler and watching transfixed by the real live porn being played out in front of me, to going through training classes with my Grandfather's second in command to learn the proper way to perform various sexual acts to maximize the clients pleasure and the clubs for profits, to being beaten for offering sexual favors to the store clerk in exchange for grocery money when my mom left her purse at home, it was just my life. I experienced all of this at the hands of my family members before I was 6 years old.

My Grandfather died just before my 6th birthday. At the same time my dad's job transferred him to a different city, these events effectively ended my trafficking experience, yet for many years afterwards, I lived a double life. One life was the good upstanding moral Christian daughter my parents wanted, the other was the sex addicted person who sought after pornography and sexually explicit books and created sexual fantasies in my head.

When I was 16 my health teacher gave us a good touch/bad touch speech and said the word incest. She also included a handout of possible indicators that one might be an incest survivor. I obviously met all of the criteria but my father was not the perpetrator and my Grandfather and Grandmother were deceased so I just brushed it off as being empathetic rather than applying to me specifically.

Then when I turned 21 and moved out on my own I decided I was tired of the double life so I sought counselling for my addictions to sex and alcohol. I was also sexually assaulted by a man I trusted and had known for many years. The sexual assault opened up the floodgates of incest memories and I had my first flashback.

I vividly remember the moment when my counsellor brought up incest and the criteria for being a survivor, which again I fit to a tee. I told her my dad and I are cool and she said OK so tell me about your other male relatives. That was a novel concept but I just started listing off relatives and I when I said my grandfathers and uncles names the light bulb went off and it was truly enlightening. Finally I was able to connect the dots and understand that I was not crazy, confused or over empathizing with my fellow survivors.

From that point on I spent years delving into AA and AL-ANON, working the 12 steps, and talking to counsellors. I began my spiritual journey too, God was now truly a higher power and someone I could lean on for support when my non-existent will power failed to keep me on the sober track. During this time I got serious about my college education and earned a Bachelor's Degree in social work with an emphasis on domestic violence and women's history.

Between the ages of 30 and 35 I worked in various areas of the social work field and became politically active in my local community. I then decided to go back to school for my Masters Degree in social work. During this time I was still focusing on the domestic violence aspects of my story and I also began my foray into research and Gerontology.

As I pursued my education and began my internship with my state coalition against domestic violence I really began to see the strong connection between being an incest survivor and then picking up an adult partner who was physically and/or sexually abusive. I say this because now I understand a big chunk of grooming is to convince the child that love and sex are synonymous and because the perpetrator is a relative, that larger society

11

says the child must love, respect and obey, then how is a child supposed to know that there is a different narrative around love and sex available to them when they grow up?.

During my internship I met many strong powerful women and helped set up assistance for these women to find community resources to get back on their feet after breaking out of domestic violence situations. That was also my first experience with understanding what trafficked women looked like, but then as I said I met a woman who was being actively trafficked and controlled by her pimp.

As she and I built our relationship and rapport I began to fully realize that yes, my grandfather sexually abused me and my grandmother, but he also traded me to his friends and had me pose for pictures and had me perform sex acts for money. It wasn't so much that I didn't know these things happened to me or working as a prostitute, it was that I just didn't connect the two ideas of prostitution and trafficking together.

Thus I found myself dealing with this weird trifecta of labels, incest survivor, sex worker and human trafficking survivor.

In many ways it was like a ah ha moment when my counsellor told me to broaden my definition of incest to include my extended male relatives. There was a sense of the left shoe being the incest survivor and the right shoe being the trafficking survivor and then both feet walking this sexual abuse survivor path.

Now I'm at the place of saying brave women and men have kicked the door down and finally started to open that door to enable an open public discussion about sexual harassment via the Me Too Campaign, and human trafficking survivors have also come into the National and International spotlight with the changing legislation around how internet sites can post adds essentially selling women and children to the highest bidder. Thus it's time for incest survivors to come out of the shadows and speak the truth.

Mother
Jesse Hepburn 2018

If it's not one thing...it's your mother. Unless like me, you were raised by your Grandmother, who was trying to atone for her sins as a mother so she started over with another generation.
To be fair my grandmother, mother and I did share a monster in common, in the form of my Grandfather.

The problem is my mother is so far in denial she should be an Egyptian citizen whereas I took a more Buddhist zen approach and called him a true mother f****r he is/was.

Speaking of that....I am repeatedly asked do I think he did this to my mother too? but sadly mom's denial of the facts about any of this or commiseration about what was obviously a shared experience.

I think the worse part though is the pain in my heart that comes from grieving for the child I was...whilst also grieving for the Peter
Panesqe child my mother is.

She just never grew up.

I have seen my recovery through to the end and I am ready to begin living my life again as a survivor.
My mom on the other hand is still living in a childhood land that she will go to extreme violent ends to defend against reality or adulthood breaches.

It's a strange experience to parent your parent. It's mentally and physically exhausting to remember to switch hats so you don't get beaten or scratched.

It's hard to remember you can speak the truth to others but to speak the truth to your own mother gets you ruthlessly hurt.

The pain is there because we did share the same horrors. Weirdly and sadly my earliest memories are of being told that I was not your mother, and thus it was I that actually showed an aptitude for being a prostitute and didn't need to be beaten or psychologically tricked into submission.

It breaks my heart into pieces to write this about how my mother was treated and to know she will never let me discuss this with her or show her how to get on the survivor/recovery path to wholeness.

It's a mess because self preservation means I have to see her less and close her out more, when I long for her to be my mother and share with her the victory shout that comes with being a published author and survivor.

So with a nod to my Freud figurine hanging from my car's rear view mirror. Yes it's definitely all about your mother. Yet no matter what, you will always love her.

....

Chapter Notes

I was coming toward the end of my research for this book when I met Jesse through the Rockstarr Ministries Facebook Group.

Rockstarr is a group of survivors and those who are empathetic of their cause.

Truth be known I wasn't really looking to add anymore content to the book as I had several interviews lined up, however I came across the "Dear Grandfather" letter and instantly knew that I needed to include Jesse and her story and work.

Jesse is an American campaigner and activist who can always be seen supporting the many survivors on the various human trafficking pages.

The thing that struck me about Jesse is the fact that she is open, honest and often frank about her thoughts and beliefs about the cause. It is through this and our mutual passion for survivors' justice that we have agreed to co-author a book together in the not so distant future. We have hopes that both this and the future project may do well on both sides of the pond.

I, Matryoshka

My name is Anya and I was born and raised in a small town just outside of Budapest, Hungary.

Both of my parents were hard working but we had very little money. Don't get me wrong, we did not live in complete poverty and my father always put food on the table, but the bills would always mount up and we had very little to get by.

My brother Seb was very little help, 13 years older than me and he hung about in the wrong crowds. He would always bring trouble to the door, mostly local debt collectors who would be looking for money because he owed them, mostly for drugs. He was in and out of Drug Rehabilitation Centres from the age of 17.

When I was 7 years my mother passed away of breast cancer and the bills began to mount. My father was left devastated and unable to cope, so he found his solace in alcohol, it was not long before he lost his job and fell into depression and with my brother's drug use, went out of control. So there I was, not even 8 and left to look after my father and my family home, I had to grow up fast. I knew that if I were to be taken into the care system we would lose everything and I would be taken away from my father, so I had to put on a brave face and pretend like everything was OK.

By now, my brother's lifestyle had landed him a life sentence in prison for murder.

It was on a visit with him, just after my 8th birthday that I met Stephan. Stephan was an acquaintance of my brother and a local business owner. Upon leaving the prison with my father, Stephan introduced himself and handed a business card to my father. He complimented me on my looks, told me that I was a beautiful young girl and that he was 100 percent positive that he could find me modeling work which would be well paid and that also if my father agreed, then he would be my manager and at his own personal cost, make sure that all of our financial worries go away, and whilst under his care my father and brother would be taken care of and that I would be safe under with him, that he would treat me as his own daughter. My father of course agreed and I was more than happy to be providing for my family and to be honest it felt good to be told that I was beautiful enough to model.

Truth be known, I had always had some confidence issues about my looks. I had dark skin and a slightly overweight physical appearance. I told Stephan of this and he just smiled and said that young looking girls are the best kind of models as there were plenty of international magazines that wanted to work with us, he would always call me beautiful, make me feel special. He called me his favourite, his brown eyed beautiful girl and that made me feel so very special and loved, after all isn't that what any child needs more than anything, especially those that have felt grief and loss.

Stephan would take me for meals, buy me the finest clothes, dolls and treat me like a princess. I liked him a lot and to be honest I had a little childhood crush on him. I guess he was around 30 years old, always immaculately dressed in the best suits. He stood at around 6 foot tall, a well toned and muscular physique, beautiful jet black hair and a smile that would make you feel so warm inside. He would take me to see his friends and family and they all seemed very nice. They appeared so kind and caring especially his auntie V. She was an older well dressed and well spoken lady with gray hair. She made the most amazing meals and always made sure I was well fed. She would always make sure that I looked my best whenever I was taken to gatherings. She even let me wear a little light make up. She told me that a lady should always look her best and be at her most polite, especially around the men. She taught me how to stand, when to speak, how to speak and so on. I kind of liked it, liked the thought of being a lady. I felt so grown up.

It was not long before I was taken to my first photo shoot. I was dressed in a white dress with red flowers. My long black hair was in pig tails and I wore a beautiful silk red ribbon in my hair. Every detail was taken care of by auntie V, even down to my plain white underwear.

The car journey seemed like hours and we had set off very early in the morning. Stephan drove whilst I sat in the back with auntie V. It was dark when we left and the sun was shining when we arrived.

It was a large single story house surrounded by woodland. The main room was large with an open fire. The floor was wooden and the furniture seemed old.

We were met by a large old man with long snowy white hair and long beard, I do admit it made me smile as he reminded me of Szent Mikulas (the man you would call Santa Clause). He had a soft voice with what I learned was a British accent. He bent down and asked me my name.

"Anya" I whispered

"Well Anya, my name is Tom and I am your friend" He said as he stroked my face.

He gestured to Auntie 'V' to follow him, she gentility grabbed me by the hand. I was led into the most beautiful room I had ever seen. It was a bedroom fit for a princess. The walls were white with gold flowers embossed into the wallpaper. A large double bed sat under the window. The bed was covered in teddy bears and dolls. I was totally amazed. He saw me looking in awe and then he told me that if I did well I could take any one thing from the room.

At the right hand side of the bed on a dark wooden unit stood a beautiful large Matryoshka (a Russian nesting doll). I pointed to her and he nodded and smiled. I love her, I still do. In fact I still have her after all these years.

He told me all I had to do was sit on the bed and play with the toys whilst he took pictures of me for a magazine. This made me happy, and modeling seemed easy and fun. I played for a while whilst he took pictures of me, auntie V just stood next to him, her arms folded as usual. When he finished he took the Matryoshka and handed her to me and smiled.

On the way out he asked Stephan if he could give me a little kiss and hug. Stephan nodded and he came down on his knees and pulled me in for a hug. I guess it felt nice as he wrapped his arms around me. Then he kissed me softly on the lips. I had never been kissed like that before on the lips, by anyone but my mother. His beard was coarse and kind of irritated my face, yet as auntie V had taught me, I just smiled and said thank you.

Over the coming months there were several more shoots. The last one I remember because I was just in a pair of flowered knickers. I thought this was strange when the rather large sweaty American photographer asked me to do it. I didn't really want to do it but I did not want to disappoint Stephan and auntie V, plus she said it was ok and for a children's underwear catalogue.

It was not long after this when my father died of a heart attack and because my brother was in prison, I was going to be sent to an orphanage. Stephan and auntie V would have none of it and took me into their home so I would not be alone.

The day of my father's funeral came, which they paid for. Auntie V stood behind me, dressed in black whist Stephan held my hand, stroking it softly with his finger, comforting me, I felt so loved and safe.

Several days later Stephan took me to a small wooded area where there were several male photographers and a young looking, very pretty blonde lady in a suit. Stephan told me that this would be a little different to what I was used to and that I would be naked because it was a shoot for a book about child body development and that by doing this, I would be helping medical science and educating people in the process. This made me a little more at ease because who wouldn't want to help medical science?

Stephan undressed me and when I was naked he just looked me up and down and smiled. He looked at me and ran his hand down my face. "You know I love you don't you" He said softly and I nodded. He kissed me softly on the lips then walked me over to the photographers, turned and walked away.

I didn't really understand what I was doing. I was told to do lots of different poses touching myself in different, intimate places. It seemed like a long time and the whole thing confused me. My ears were filled with the sound of mumbling and camera shutters, so to concentrate I focused on the sound of the birds, this was calming.

The cameras stopped for a moment and Stephan walked over to me and came down on one knee and softly spoke.

"OK beautiful girl, this is the last shot today, I promise. I need you to do one last thing. I need you to lay on your back on the floor and open your legs as far as you can".

I did not understand, he could see the confusion sat upon my face. He took a long breath and smiled.

"OK, you know how we are making a book about the development of children. Yes?"

I nodded.

"Well we need to show between the legs, so some older children can understand the difference between boy and girl, do you understand?"

Again I nodded.

" We also need you to touch yourself down there, open it up as far as you can so we can see everything, remember this is for science, for education, once this is finished I will take you to buy a beautiful dress, any dress you want. You like to look beautiful don't you?"

I was silent and scared.

Not saying anything he took my hand and walked me over. He put one hand behind my head and the other on the back of my knees and laid me down. He leaned over me and whispered

"I love you, you know that, I love you like a daughter".

I smiled, "Do you love me, tell me you love me" he said. "I do" I replied.

"Then say it, say you love me".

"I love you" I whispered, he smiled.

20

The last words he said have always stuck with me, I will never forget.

"Don't you ever forget it!"

and with those words he parted my legs and gave a large grin. As he went to get up he kissed me between my legs, he had never done this before, but he would do it many times after.

You have to understand, I didn't know any different, I didn't know what it was, I believed everything he told me, why would I not. Looking back, I can see that this was the point that things really began to turn.

Anyway I digress, Stephan nodded to the photographers as he walked away, grinning, and the photos began again. It didn't seem like a short while, it felt like a day, laying there bearing all at the age of 10. I didn't not want to disappoint Stephan, I wanted to educate the children like he told me. I feel sick just thinking about it, I know in my heart that the abuse began mentally from the moment we first met, but this is when I now realize it became physical, well at least with Stephan anyway.

We arrived back at auntie V's mid afternoon and I was pretty worn out and didn't feel too well after the shoot. Stephan told me to go to my room and relax for a little while and then he would take me to buy a beautiful dress with auntie V. He suggested that I take a bath, "Maybe that will make you feel a bit better" he said, he smiled as auntie V nodded. As he left auntie V spoke.

"Come child, I will run you a bath"

She said softly and led me to the bathroom. I wondered for years if she knew what he was going to do or whether she just constantly cleaned up after every on the spot psychotic, fucked up decision he made. Whether she did or not is irrelevant, the fact that she enabled him is just as bad as what he did to me, what he made me do and the life they both pushed me into for their own gain.

21

There I was splashing away as any child of my age would, innocently playing. I didn't even blink when Stephan walked in, I was used to it. He would often come and sit on the toilet and talked to me whilst I bathed, in fact he would often wash me, I saw nothing wrong with it, my father often did the same.

He seemed different, a little distant. I just thought he may have been drinking but I had seen that before so I just thought he may have felt a little unwell. He told me that I should get out of the bath and get dry before I caught a cold. He just sat there intently watching me as I dried myself.

When I had finished he followed me into my bedroom and sat on the edge of my bed. I was about to get dressed and he told me just to leave my towel wrapped around me and to just sit on the bed for a moment. I thought nothing of it and did as I was asked.

"Sit there a moment beautiful girl and I will be back in a moment" he said. He got up and left the room and there I sat like a good girl until he returned a few moments later.

When he came back he was holding a glass with cloudy liquid in it. He told me to drink it, that it would stop me from getting ill. So I drank it and he smiled, why would I not?

It tasted bitter and wanted to stop, but he just put his hand to the bottom of the glass and made sure I drank it all.

"I don't like it" I said.
"Shhh, it is good for you" he replied.

It wasn't long before I started to feel funny, a little sick, sleepy and light headed. He just smiled and laid me down on the bed, opening my towel as he did so. I wanted to protest but I couldn't. I wanted to speak but the words would not come out. I felt so distant from my own mind, yet I knew everything that went on. I could not move no matter how much I would try, it was like my body was asleep, yet I was awake.

22

There I lay, helpless and naked as all I could do was watch as he removed his trousers. He parted my legs and began to kiss me there. It hurt and began to get sore because of his stubble. Then without warning he parted my legs and laid over me, he was kissing my face, I had never known him like this before. He was like a monster.

The next thing I felt was an almighty pain beginning between my legs and into my stomach. It hurt so much. I wanted to scream, to cry out in pain, but I could not. I remember my tears blinding me, my own words choking me as I tried to cry out. The pain just got worse, it hurt more and more and he turned into more of a monster.

I remember very little after that. I don't know whether I passed out in pain or through the sickening dizziness.

When I awoke auntie V was sat at the end of the bed, I could barely move. I hurt so much. Auntie V just sat there holding my hand, smiling. Yet this was a different smile, a smile with pain hidden behind it. For a long time after well, until recently to be honest, I hated her for it. How dare she, in fact how could she even attempt to hide it. It was an abomination, the things they subjected me to, the things that would be done to me in the coming years, and she was a part of it.

The hate I had for so many people, for everyone who had a part in my captivity, anyone who ever touched me, took my photo and took away every last ounce of my fucking innocence, well the hate filled me for such a long time, it took me to a place that no one should ever have to see or go. She told me that I could never tell anyone of what had happened or I would be put into the orphanage and I would end up on drugs or dead in the system. She told me that this was normal in many families, that it would keep happening and I would get used to it. Someday my body would pay the bills, that I should be grateful. She also said that it would get easier and my body would get used to it.

One thing I forgot to say was that I loved my Matryoshka, She sat pride of place on my bedside drawers looking at me. I don't know why but she gave me so much comfort.

Every day for weeks he raped me and when he finished he would tell me he loved me, he would demand I told him I loved him back, and if I didn't he would do it faster and harder until in my own tears, my own agony I would tell him just to make it stop.

He had raped me so many times that the sex no longer hurt and I had gotten used to it. It was more of a discomfort now due to only being a small frame. Then all of a sudden it stopped.

For month after month, every night I expected it but it did not come. Every time I would walk past him I would expect to be grabbed, but he didn't, he just smiled. This I would learn was the calm before the storm because what happened next would change me forever.

It was my 10th birthday and auntie V had a party in the afternoon for me. Well I say party, she gave me a doll, cake and soft drinks. I was sat at the kitchen table when Stephan arrived home with a present in hand. He handed it to me and told me to open it in my room later. He told me he had arranged for someone to do my makeup for me, to make me look stunning.

It was at that moment that dread filled my heart, deep inside I knew something was coming and it made me feel sick to the bone. I had recently started puberty and had begun to develop breasts and a small amount of bodily hair. It was confusing enough and now all this. I didn't want a party, I just wanted to curl into a ball and die, even the orphanage sounded good.

It was late in the afternoon when Selina arrived. She was a beautiful golden haired girl in her mid 20s. She wore a tight red dress and she spoke with a soft German accent. She seemed very nice, she told me she had come to make me up, to be my friend, to give me advice.

Auntie V told her to take me to my room, so she gently took my hand and told me to lead the way. I sat on the edge of my bed holding Matryoshka whilst she knelt behind me, brushing my long black hair slowly and softly.

"So tell me Anya, what has he made you do?"

"What do you mean?" I naively answered

"Does he touch you, does he make you do things to him?
Does he rape you?"

She knew the answer by the look I gave her, I cradled Matryoshka close to my chest and she could see the comfort I took in her. The words she said to me would stick with me for the rest of my life. This conversation, These words I would and still do live my life by. I remember it word for word, I would like to share them with you, and if any brave young boys or girls who are trapped in an abusive situation may take comfort, or anyone like me who have finally escaped may find some solace in them.

"What is this thing you hold so close for comfort?"

"Matryoshka" I answered.

A puzzled look sat upon her face. So I showed her doll inside doll, inside doll and so on and placed them side by side on my bedside cabinet.

A line of Matryoshka from big to small. She smiled a painful smile.
She began.

"When I was not much older than you I had a doll, her name was Annie. She was old and belonged to my sister before me and my mother before her. She was old, but well kept. She was made of the softest wool. My Oma, I believe you would call her Nagymama (Grandmother) made her when my mother was a little girl.

Anna was my best friend in the whole world, I would tell her everything. All of my hopes, fears, dreams and when the day came I began to tell her my secrets. She would go everywhere with me. When I went to bed she would lay with me. I took great comfort in her company.

When my father would come in the nighttime, as he did every night from the age of 8, I would hold her hand. The first time he did it I screamed into her. When he finished I held her. She did not judge, she could not speak. When I got used to it, whilst he did it, I would look at her, hold her in my hand, because no matter how much pain or discomfort I was in she was

25

always be willing to let me squeeze her, as hard as I wished. She could not feel pain like I did.

Stephan and my father are the same and I know he will do to you what he did to me, and he will do this tonight at your party. We are both slaves, neither of us are able to escape at this moment. Other men will come, he will sell your body. You may not understand at the moment but we are both trapped. We cannot escape this yet, but we will one day. When you are older you will know.

Look at your nesting dolls, the smallest one is you at this time. You cannot yet control what they do but like your Matryoshka you can surround yourself in something else, build yourself another skin. Your body will change, it belongs to him, but your mind never will. Put all of yourself into Matryoshka. Your hopes, dreams, goals, secrets and pain.

When they come, the men and women, yes even the women will want to do things to you, they will make you do things to them, then put it all into your nesting doll. Your Matryoshka is you at the centre, the skins around her are the things you use to survive, to feel better, to protect the littlest doll, because that tiny thing encased in everything else is hope and don't ever let go of hope.

There will be many men tonight that will do things to you, who will have you do things to them. You will feel some pain but remember it will end. These people want your body, your innocence, they will think they own you because they have paid. They don't, they may use your body but your mind belongs to you.

I have to make you look older, with makeup, with your clothes and underwear. Like you, I have no choice, they would kill me even if they knew I was saying this to you.

Protect your hope with every ounce of strength you have, because if you lose hope you may as well be dead."

Tears ran down her face as she held back the grief of her own words. I could not, will not, ever blame her for the situation I was in, she was

26

nothing like auntie V. She was just as much a hostage as I was. I heard that Selina was found dead of a drugs overdose several months later. Part of me wonders whether it was because she lost her hope or because they found out what she said to me. I guess I will never know.

I looked in the mirror as Selina left, I looked so much older yet my body was so young. Everything about me at that moment was so confusing. My face looked older, my lips so red, my cheeks roses with makeup. I was dressed in frilly black knickers and a small bra that was a little too large for my developing breasts. Toilet tissue was used to fill it out. On top of that I wore a tight black dress.

I was paraded around the room in front of 20 or so men. Some old and gray, some younger like Stephan. I was introduced and gave small talk like I had learned to.

Now what I will tell you next about what happened will disturb you, that is if you are not disturbed to madness by my story already. I have no wish to offend anyone who is hearing my story, but I feel I need to be frank, honest and described the things that happened to me, that happens to others, to educate you , to show you the life we are forced to live. You may get upset and angry, and if you do, well good, I really hope my life makes you want to do something to help people like me.

My agreement with the author of this book is that he takes care not to censor too many of my words, too much of my story. I want you to know what has and what will happen to people like me.

My story may or may not be the most painful to read in this book, in fact to be honest my life as a sexual slave could be seen as easy compared to some.

There are those who suffer worse than I did. Anyway I shall continue.

After I was paraded around the room Stephan took me back to my room and made me undress and wash away the makeup whilst he watched. I did not understand why he would dress me like this and in such a short time make me take it off, I dared not ask.

Once my face was clean and naked he forced me to perform oral sex on him right there in the bathroom. I knew from every other time that I could not say no, complain or resist or he would just do it harder, all I could do was submit to what he wanted me to do. This wasn't something he hadn't made me do before. I was used to it by now, it was always the least painful part, however this time was different. He would usually make me stop so he could fully rape me and it would be over relatively quickly, yet this time he gripped my head so firmly I could not move. Every time I tried to pull away the harder he would pull my head closer to him. I began to gag, to choke and the more I did the more of a monster he became. It hurt so much, he became angry as my stifled screams and gags made me want to puke. He pushed me off with force, this was unlike him, even though he raped me before he was often gentle and only hurt me or got faster if I resisted. This was like someone else. He growled and snarled as I vomited in the toilet. He didn't even let me finish coughing before he grabbed my hair and raped me from behind right there over the toilet. Pushing my head into the bowl, pulling my hair and raping me harder than he'd ever done before. As I screamed into the toilet he just got more sadistic. At one point He pushed my head so far down the toilet my feet barely touch the ground. He even flushed the toilet as he pushed my face into the porcelain.

When he finished he threw me across the room into the shower and pissed all over my face. It made me so sick and he just laughed whilst I cried. I had been raped so many times it didn't even really hurt for that long. I was used to it but this made me feel dirty, used and horrible. He told me that this wasn't even the start, my birthday surprise hadn't even began. He ordered me to get a shower, that I was dirty and that I made him sick.

"Clean yourself up whore and then back downstairs naked, do you understand" He barked.

I just nodded and he left, trying desperately not to show weakness, holding back my tears.

I felt so sick, confused and hurt. It was not the fact that he raped me, I was used to that, it was the fact that this man who I genuinely loved, the man who was so kind and generous had turned into this monster so quickly.

28

Even before, when he raped me, he never hurt me like this, he always smiled and after he would often buy me things. As I have said, the pain of sex no longer hurt, it was the pain of the man turning into a demon right in front of me. Now I know why Selina had told me to hold on to hope, because it was fading fast.

Anyway, I did as I was told, got clean and walked into the room naked. When I got in there he was standing there naked with 7 other men who were also naked and my heart filled with dread.

I will not go into great detail about what happened next as I have already gone into detail about other instances, and I fear it may be too much for you to bear. Needless to say they took it in turns to rape me one by one, made me do unspeakable things to them all. They did this most of the night until the early hours of the morning. I was exhausted and in so much pain.

Again, the rapes would stop for months at a time whilst I was allowed to heal. Occasionally he would come in the night and make me give him oral sex, but this was tame to the things he had subjected me to in the past.

When I did heal he would sell my body to his friends and the gang rapes would not happen again for a few years. Occasionally he would sit and watch whilst a friend of his raped me, but that hope would always remain in my Matryoshka. In fact, just as Selina had said I had become Matryoshka myself. It was a good way to survive, to remain myself whilst my body was being used.

By the time I had reached 16 I think I looked too old for him, he no longer came in the night, he no longer raped me, he just sold me to his friends, to his clients. I was already fully developed. Yet I felt so old for one still so relatively so young.

He would let me go to town with an escort, he let the reins go a little. He would have me visit men at their home to service them although I never took money because they had already paid either with cash or favour.

This became less and less until it had stopped. This would result in the final time that he would rape me. I think, No! I know he only did it to mark me as his property, not that I wasn't already. He had been raping me for years, holding me captive. I was already his property, I had been trapped for years and I saw no escape.

As I said, he had not touched me for several years, I suppose you would say that he pimped me out to his friends for years. I had been in the bath and when I came out he was standing at my door, he had been drinking. I knew the score, I knew what was going to happen so I just let my towel drop by the bed and lay down. As he staggered towards me I thought he was too drunk, I thought I could control him, I was wrong.

He forced himself on top of me and looked into my eyes and smiled. He put his hand on my throat and tightened his grip, all I could do was grab his wrist.

"You are nothing but a whore, you disgust me" he said through angry gritted teeth.

"You belong to me, and you will start paying your way, you are going to work on the street, you belong to me".

I could do nothing but fight for air. He flipped me over and fumbled around his trousers. He bit me, slapped me round my head and face as he raped me anally. It hurt so much; all I could do was cry in pain into the pillow. He sadistically moved the pillow and yanked my hair and head back as he went harder. He laughed at my screaming and crying, punched me in the ribs, in my side. It seemed to last for hours. When he finished he dragged me off of the bed. Now on the floor he slapped me, kicked me.

He lit a cigarette as I lay on the floor a bloody, crying mess. He took one long drag from his cigarette and put it out on my inner thigh. It was agony like I had never felt before.

It wasn't long before he sent me to work on the streets. There are many horror stories I could tell you about those times but that would be a book in itself. Perhaps one day I will find the strength and courage to write my memoirs, however for now this will have to do.

30

I was a street worker for almost 20 years. I had thoughts of suicide every day, but I knew if I did kill myself Stephan would have beaten me.

When I was 35, Stephan suffered a fatal heart attack and I knew I could finally be free. On the day he died I fled the town, never looking back, only looking forward to a new life away from sexual slavery.

I made my way through Europe working only when I needed money and had saved enough to finally get a passport and buy a ticket to England. I have been here nearly 20 years now. I have a good life, my own business and live in a Civil Partnership with my partner of 8 years.

Chapter Notes

I was introduced to Anya through a mutual acquaintance within the fairly local church/writers network. Anya was my first interview for this book, hence the reason I decided to open the book with her story and with that in mind, of all the personal stories I have heard in compiling this book, I must say that this one has really hit a nerve with me. All of the testimonies have affected me in a profound and heartbreakingly difficult way but for some reason this has caused me to shed the most tears.

Before I started the interview with Anya I asked her what name name she would like to be known as in the book. She smiled and looked at her partner who replied

"Call her Anya, Anya means mother and although she has barely known one she has a certain way about her. She is caring and beautiful, kind and considerate, gentle and generous. She is like a mother, so please call her Anya".

This stuck with me through the whole interview, and still sticks with me today. Often I was brought to tears and had to stop the interview to compose myself and my thoughts. I am still new to this whole world of writing and interviewing so I really got caught up in what she was saying, her words brought heartbreak, grief and anger. When I did, she showed concern for me and I knew that the name that was chosen and the reason behind it were bang on the mark. On several occasions her voice would break, a tear would fall. The strength of that woman truly astounds me.

I don't really wish to describe her through the fear that may contribute to breaking her anonymity. I made a promise to her, in fact everyone whom I interviewed, to protect their anonymity.
I will however confess that I have nothing but admiration for this strong, beautiful warrior.

She carried a smile almost throughout. I know that smile, I have used it myself. Like most who have lived through major trauma, she carries her pain in her eyes and naturally attempts to hide it behind a smile. This isn't intentional, it is a learned automatic response.

To use such a simple thing as a Matryoshka to survive such a horrific past and project her pain and suffering into that and still hold that object in such high regard is astounding.

I myself have used many different techniques to deal with my own past, my own trauma. This mostly involved drugs and bad behaviour. It took me near death to even begin to deal with mine but I am aware we all have our own different strategies and mechanisms to deal with our own personal demons. It did not take me too long to realise that she had more demons to deal with than most.

In The Family

Tony

Do you know what it is like to not feel as if you are human, to be treated like a product, an object?

I do! And it is soul destroying. I was a slave in every sense of the word. I had no freedom to speak of, and even though I have long escaped the slavery they forced me into, I will never be truly free.

I never knew my father and my mother who suffered a great deal of mental illness and addiction died of a heroin overdose when I was 6 years old. Shortly after her death I was sent to live with my aunt in a small town in Texas, so everything I knew would change, in a state I did not know.

Things seemed OK when I first met my aunt. She was in her late 20s, had long, beautiful auburn hair. She seemed nice and loving.

She came across as gentle, loving and kind. I never really knew what life was like, how a mother should treat her child as I had only ever known mine in her addiction. Occasionally my mother was loving, however most of the time she would be in a drugged up mess and I was left to fend for myself, so having a kind, tactile motherly figure seemed strange.

Things were OK for a few months whist I settled in to my new home, my new life. Dan was my aunt's boyfriend. At the beginning he dropped by to introduce himself, he gave me a Catcher's Mitt and a Baseball. We even played catch for a while.

As time went on Dan would stop by more and more, he seemed so generous. He would always bring gifts and candy.

One Saturday afternoon we had been hurling a football in the yard. It could be very dusty out there so my aunt told me I needed to take a bath. My aunt bathed me whilst Dan sat on the lavatory just watching. I didn't see anything wrong with it. I didn't know any different, after all this is what families do, right? It seemed to last ages, but who was I to complain? I was getting the attention I thought I needed.

I didn't have any friends to speak of, we lived several miles away from the nearest town on a smallholding/ ranch. We only ever went into town every month or so and I would always sit in the truck whilst Dan and my aunt would get the supplies in. I would help out with feeding the cows and the horses.

Every time I helped out or played in the yard I would be told I needed to bathe, because "After all, a clean boy is a good boy" as my aunt used to say. They would take it in turns to wash me whilst the other just sat there and watched. Again, this seemed normal to me.

This went on for a year or so.

Looking back I can see where it all began. It was mid Fall and I had not long celebrated my 7th birthday. I had done my chores in the morning and was tossing and catching a tennis ball against the yard wall.

Oh I forgot to say that by now Dan had moved in with my aunt permanently.

Again I was told to bathe, yet this time was different. When Dan took me to the bathroom my aunt was already bathing. I went a little red. "Not to worry little man, get in with your aunt" Dan suggested. I was a little weary but she smiled and gestured for me to undress and get in with her. I was very nervous but she was assuring. I was 7, I had never seen a grown woman naked. I didn't know where to look and Dan caught me looking upon my aunt's breasts and smiled. Seeing my nerves my aunt moved back slightly in the tub and smiled reassuringly.

"It's ok little darlin, it's all a natural thing, the body is from God. Nothing to be ashamed or nervous of" she said, then pulled me in close and put my head into her breasts.

"See, skin is skin, soft and warm" she whispered and then let me go.

The whole time Dan stood there watching, smiling, hands in the pockets of his pants.

My aunt got out of the tub, she didn't even bother with drying herself off, she just stood there showing off her body. She smiled and wandered out of the bathroom. Dan lifted me out of the bath and said

"Come on little man let's get you dry," and led me into my aunt's bedroom to dry me off.

When we got into the bedroom my aunt was sat at the end of her bed, both of us still as naked as the day were born.

I don't really want to go into too much graphic detail, but they had me feel her breasts, stroke the hair between her legs. I don't suppose it lasted too long although it felt like an eternity to me at the time. It wasn't long before Dan led me back to my room to get me dressed.

The next time I was bathed it was Dan in the tub and my aunt watching. I couldn't say no, I didn't want to make them mad. The last time I saw an adult get mad it was my mom, and she near enough trashed the apartment.

Sure enough, same routine in reverse. Dan on the bed whilst my aunt watched. I was made to touch his penis, I really didn't like that.
This routine carried on for years.

After tub time, after the touching I would be left in my room. I remember thinking the noises that would come from their room were the darnedest thing. It sounded painful, I dared not ask, I dared not say a word.

Things were taken up a notch when I hit 9 years old. A new routine came into place alongside the old one. They called it the mimic me game. This would take place after tub time.

They would touch me in a place and I would have to do the same to them. This wasn't just with hands, it was with mouth too. I didn't like it none too much at first, but they began to incorporate tickling. How can a game be that bad if it involves tickling eh? However, when all was finished, back to my room and the noises began again.

These routines carried on for a year or so I guess. I wasn't quite 11 but my body had begun to change. I don't mean hair or anything yet but I had started getting erections. My aunt had noticed it at tub time. She had been washing me in that area. She smiled and said to Dan

"Awww, our little boy is growing up".
They both had an indescribable look hidden in their smiles.

The games kicked up a notch and the mimic game was changed so they would excite me enough to get an erection and take turns kissing me there. This is now what I realize as the beginnings of oral sex.

The mimic game became even more sinister (as if it wasn't already) and I would have to copy what they did to each other. This included simulating sex with my aunt. I say simulating because I was still of such a small frame. I am in no doubt that had I been a little larger in frame they would have had me having full sex earlier than I did.
They kept me home schooled, if you can call it that. There was very little education to speak of apart from sexual.

My life consisted of playing catch, tossing a football, shooting hoops, tub time and what they now called play time.

By the time I hit 12 I had started puberty and my body began to develop. It was at this time the games stopped, well they stopped making them games, calling them games. This was full sexual contact. They became less kind and more demanding. I was at their beck and call whenever they wanted, so pretty much 24/7. It was then that their friends began to visit. I would be made to call each and everyone auntie or uncle.

I was pretty much confined to my room. I had a TV bolted to the wall that showed films and TV programs, most of them were family films and kids programs. The electric socket on the wall was boxed off and padlocked so I could not turn it off if I tried. I was not allowed clothes and all I had was a blanket to cover myself.

My room was in the basement of the house. There was a CCTV Camera in the left hand corner of the room. I knew then that I was a slave, that I was not free. Watched 24/7. The only time the door would be opened would be to feed me, or to take me into the yard for air. This was usually in the evening, I was still naked as they didn't ever have to worry about anyone they didn't want seeing me, as we were pretty secluded from the outside world. Dan had built a toilet in the room. No walls just a basic porcelain toilet in the corner.

I knew when it was going to happen, when someone was going to come. The channel would change on the TV set and pornography would be shown. The door would open and someone would come to abuse me. The men would come to sodomize me, to make me do things to them. The only women that ever came were my aunt and an older large lady. I would be made to give them oral and have full sex with them. Not one person ever used a condom when they would sodomize me. I wouldn't be allowed a condom when I was forced to have sex with my aunt and her friend. This would not stop until I was around 15 I guess. I didn't have birthdays anymore.

My life was pretty much constant sexual abuse by then. Person after person, day after day, nearly all day with only a few hours of sleep at night. I could barely get off of the bed anymore due to constantly being sodomized.

I guess they got cocky and had been noticed. I remember the day that it happened. I don't know what time, it was dark I guess and the door was broken open with such a force. I just lay cowering in the bed. The police officers came in a crowd.

John was one of those officers. When he saw me he struggled to hold back the emotion. He covered me with a fresh blanket. He told me I was safe now, that no one would ever hurt me again. He spoke softly and carried me out of the room in his arms to the ambulance. He traveled with me and stayed with me for hours.

He came to visit me every day. He brought his wife and children to see me. They would eventually become my family. I later found out that after analysis of my sheets there were more than 300 semen samples and 2 vaginal fluid samples. John and his wife adopted me a couple of years later and I would finally learn what family is.

I don't believe you can ever really be free from slavery. I still have the night terrors. I still never go out unescorted (through choice). I can never truly get over the horrific life I was forced into. I will never be free from those events but I do know that I am loved.

........…..…....................................

Chapter Notes

Tony is one of several people I interviewed for this book I have not personally met or seen. I first came across Tony's story when he contacted me after seeing my plea for contributors on the various internet blogs, forums and social media platforms.

We only spoke physically the once for his interview as he had very little time and I was also conscious that I did not want to put him through too much upset.

He had a strong, stern voice that softened the further we got into the interview. There were a few times that we both had to stop and take a moment to compose ourselves.

I would keep telling him just to let me know when he needed to stop and compose. Tony was also the first male I spoke to in relation to the book so I guess it made it a little harder to digest. The heartbreaking thing is that although his was the first male story, I had been told it would not be the last.

As every interview went on I learned that there are many common factors that linked every one of these stories together.

Concrete Jungle

Aiesha

I could tell you how difficult it is growing up a mixed raced female in a predominantly black area of London.

I could tell you about living in a poor neighborhood of mainly social housing in a tower block set between tower blocks, a concrete jungle you might say. A box within a box set among boxes, but what good would that do. We live in a country where the wealthy rule and the poor may die. I believe austerity is a way of culling the stragglers and the weak.

I could tell you I was unloved as a child, that I was abused and beaten every day, but that would be a downright blatant lie. Not everyone who is exploited comes from that sort of background. It is a common myth that only these type of people are exploited. Exploitation comes in many forms and is often invisible to the naked eye.

I come from a good, God loving, hard working family. 2 loving parents who worked 7 jobs between them to put food on our table, to give my siblings and I a good start in life, to give us what we needed and sometimes what we wanted.

There is such a problem in the media about how we should look, dress and act. The best trainers, latest clothes and trends and it is rubbed in the face of the poor.

I'm sure that all these problems and many more are not just localized to London, it's a worldwide problem. Where there are poor, where there is a divide in race, in class, there is crime. There are always those who will find their feet within the crime. Drugs, weapons, knock off gear. The latest mobile phone for a fraction of the price. In those areas, there will always be Gangs and Gang culture.

Not everyone who joins a gang is of the wrong sort, not always aspiring criminals. Sometimes it's about friendship, the feeling of a family, safety (especially in numbers). Bullying happens wherever you are, especially when you are a physically weak and overweight mixed raced teen in an urban situation like I was. However, I don't really want to make this about me. I grew up and lived in that culture, not through real need apart from the safety and bullying, but through wanting to rebel, to have something different, to be respected. We can feel that respect should be a given, yet it rarely is. It is earned, and then it's not real respect, it's a pseudo respect, a mask we hide behind.

There are so many girls out there that are introduced to the culture, girls as young as 12. Sex is a big part of it. I was like these girls. I did not understand the boundaries and dangers of that kind of life.

Girls 12 maybe 13 years old giving head, believing it's normal, believing it is not rape.

IT IS !!!

Sex sells, young girls and even young boys raped sometimes several times on a daily basis. Gang initiation by sex, by rape and more often than not by several men at a time, yet what can we do. It took me years to escape.

Education is needed. We need to teach the young what is and what is not rape. What is and what is not acceptable in their personal lives and not just society. Where there are young, impressionable people there will always be someone willing to overstep the mark.
Like many, I was a slave sexually. I was not a person, I was a product, unknowingly (at first) sold into prostitution.

Remember I told you about respect, well one thing I have learned that respect begins with self, and until we learn that then we will always chase respect from others, even if that means our bodies are used to pleasure others.

Gang life isn't the way. It's following others, mimicking them. If you follow that life, if you chase it because you believe it's the only way, then you are wrong. They may tell you that you are loved, respected, family. Mark my words, surrounded by loyalty, you are not. You are a product, a means to an end. It's not family, it's everyone for themselves. They will turn on you the first chance they get.

Don't be a clone, a product. Be you.

....

Chapter Notes

Aiesha only agreed to speak to me on the condition that she could tell her story this way. She told me that maybe one day she will have the inner strength to tell her own story but was not in the position at this very moment.

She told me that she still has many unresolved issues and that maybe one day when most are resolved on a personal basis and she had built up the self confidence and self security then she would speak with me about writing her full biography.

She however did have a desire to help, a desire to educate and to be a voice for those who have lived it, those who are still living it, those who have escaped and those who may bow to the pressure and allure of Gang life.

Runaway

Finn

I loved my Dad more than anything in the world. He meant more than the world to me, and I did to him. We would do everything together, go everywhere together. So when he died my whole world fell apart.

My mam did the best she could but the loss hit her really hard and she turned to drink and the shit would hit the fan in the guise of a burly beer drinking bastard by the name of Steve. He took advantage of my mam in a time of her life when she felt loss and loneliness.

Things were alright at the start. He was a bit of a poacher, so we would always have food on the table. He wasn't too bad at the start, a bit grumpy but he treated us ok, that was until he got his feet well and truly under the fucking table, it was then he became a right horrible bastard. He loved to consume more than a couple of pints down the working men's club. He would be on the drink constantly almost all day, every day. On the rare occasion he was sober, he would be quite placid, kept his temper ok, but when tanked up he was a very volatile, angry man.

He would get handy with me, with my mam. He wasn't a small feller either, hands like a workman's shovel. He would give me a right slap if he thought I was out of line. He would slap mam harder. I used to want to protect her, but what could I do but put up with it, I was 10.

This carried on for years. When I was 16 he came home steaming drunk, lost all of his money on the slots and was in a right old mood. Mam went mad because he spent her rent money. He got handy and gave her a proper hiding. I went to jump in and he kicked the living shit out of me. Yet mam still protected that bastard, so I ran away. Took me a fair few days, but 1 walked the sidings and hard shoulder of the M62, diving into the odd field if I saw the law. It wasn't too long before I ended up Manchester way.

I'd do a bit of begging and stealing to keep myself fed.

After a while I ended up sleeping outside of Manchester Piccadilly station and would make my way to Victoria if I got moved on.

After a few weeks I found myself with a heroin habit and my life went rapidly downhill. I ended up on the rob everyday just to feed my habit. Rarely would I have enough to pay my debts, let alone buy food.

I was sat at the top end of Canal Street in Manchester, begging when this bloke around 60 odd years old came up to me and asked me how old I was. I told him I was 16 and he then asked me if I wanted to earn a bit of easy cash. "How" I said. He then proceeded to tell me he would give me £50 if I let him give me oral sex. Not going to lie, I went absolutely mental, pushing him down the street, screaming at him that I wasn't gay and how dare he even think of asking a young boy that, you dirty old cunt. He just smiled and said that one day I would take him up on the offer and that it would be £30 and no more. He just walked away laughing. I was fucking fuming, I'm not gay, I never would be.

It was only a matter of a few hours later and I had began to rattle badly. I couldn't think straight, I just needed a hit.

I thought of doing a street robbery but couldn't keep my hands steady enough. The thing about heroin is that it makes you constipated so when withdrawal sets in then you really need to crap badly. So badly that you could soil yourself there and then through diarrhoea.

I ran over to the public toilets on Piccadilly station and ran into the first cubicle and my guts dropped. I was in agony, rattling.

I looked down and saw two pairs of feet in there. Noises of approval going a goodun, if you know what I mean. I stumbled out of the stall and hit the floor just as the cubicle door next to me opened. A young lad not much older than me and you guessed it, old dirty git.

He leaned over spiking at me as I rattled on the bog floor. "Hello mate" he muttered,

"Offer is there £15 for a blow job". I could barely get out my words and forced them trough gritted teeth.

"You said £30".

"Aye, I did that but I've just emptied the young lad, need to empty myself, so I'll tell ya what, I'll let you empty me, you know what I mean lad".

I knew all too well that in desperation I would have to nosh the dirty old sod off. I was in so much pain I would have done pretty much anything right there to get a hit.

"You are no good to anyone like this, let alone me, come on for God's sake, let's get you up and sorted" he said.

So, he helped me up and led me to his car, I was proper clucking, I couldn't have blamed him if he had left me there. I vaguely remember losing the limited contents of my stomach right there on the backseat of his car. Don't think the old git was too happy.

He took me into a rather posh ground floor flat where several blokes sat around smoking and sipping tea. That's right, bloody tea.

I was taken into a back bedroom with a double bed. It was rather Cushy, if I do say so myself. I was stripped down. I swear to God I thought I was gonna get gang raped right there and then. I was sat up on the bed and old dirty git, whose name I would later find out was Glen and his rather large hairy biker looking feller set up some works. It wasn't a lot, but it was enough gear to bring me round a little while later so I could function.

Of course, it goes without saying that I would find all of this out after I was medicated, if you get my drift.

When my head was straight I was led to a rather plush looking bathroom where a bath had already been run for me. I was told by the bear to get cleaned up. He left a dressing gown and a towel, he took my clothes. I won't lie, it was the nicest and longest bath I have ever had.

When I had finished I walked into the bedroom to find a pair of jeans and a plain white t-shirt waiting for me. I got dressed and found my way to the living room where they were all still smoking, still sipping tea.
So the bear perks up,

"Alrite lad, sit yersen down and relax, Glen has gone to the chippy to get your belly full. Them clothes will do you till yours are washed eh".

I just nodded nervously, I was in a strange place with people I didn't know, I was on edge and wanted to run but couldn't. I must have been proper shaking because the bear piped up again.

"Bloody hell lad, no need to be nervous, we won't hurt you, you are safe here, don't worry and chill out".

I was trying to hold back my words, stifle myself but I was absolutely shitting a brick and unable to hold back. I bleated out

"Safe, bleeding safe! you are going to gang rape me and you are telling me I'm safe".

Well the room erupted with laughter which got me angrier through embarrassment. Again the bear pipes up.

"We're not going to gang rape you, silly boy. Nobody will touch you without your permission. We will get you fed, keep you medicated if that's what you want, no debt, our gift to you. When Glen gets back we will have a chat and make you an offer, give you a job and a roof over your head. If you decide you don't want to take us up on the offer then you are free to go with your clothes and a full belly. Now have a joint and relax lad".

Truth be told, I didn't know who to trust, what to think. To be honest I was a very naive lad with trust issues. It all seemed too good to be true. Free clothes, free bed, free food and free drugs. There had to be a catch, and of course there was.

I should also tell you that I was still a virgin in every sense of the word. Well to me and my lapsed Catholic upbringing virginal meant innocent,

48

and well I was far from that. I had never even had sex education because mam kept me off school that day, let alone seen a dirty magazine and I knew what dirty old Glen wanted. I had never seen or touched a todger that was not my own so I knew that when he got back things may well and truly go south, literally!.

So, Glen gets back with fish and chips and these weirdos all sit smiling watching me wolf down my dinner. Belly full and an aperitif of a dragon to chase, they asked me to tell my life story. Whatever floats your boat eh. So I told them, I dunno why I opened up but I did. Well when I told them I was a virgin the bear's face lit up.

Did you ever see a cartoon where the character sees potential in something and you see the dollar sign in the eyes followed by the Ching Ching noise ? Well I swear if that was possible it would have happened to the hairy bearesqe bleeder.

"Two Grand, as and when you need it, in cash or in gear, or both" The bear said.

A look of confusion must have overtaken my face because I still didn't know what for and the only words I could get out were

"You what?"

"Two grand in gear and cash, as and when you need or want it, for one night of sex with me. You do what you are comfortable with and we stop" he said.

It was more money than I had ever heard or dreamed of. There I was a young, homeless heroin addict, far from home, sat in a posh flat being offered more money than I had ever heard of, just to have sex with a man. Well my mam always told me that she would disown me if I ever became gay, but I wouldn't be gay if I was being paid for it, if she didn't know about it, after all I had run away so that didn't make me gay right ?.

I must have gone over that scene, that offer a million times since. I used to think, to believe, that I had to say yes that things may have been different.

Yet knowing what I know now, living the life that I have lived, I know that I was fooling myself into believing my own lies. I know that either way I would have been theirs no matter what. I just think they were looking for an easy way. They had no intention to let me go and the easy way would have been voluntarily subservient.

I declined the offer as respectfully as I thought I could, I thought, I believed, they were straight up. How wrong could I be?

"Ok" said the bear, "please just stay and have a dig on us and we will see you on your way" he followed.

Note: (A dig is an injection of heroin)
I had never in my life turned down free drugs, I never did until I found sobriety. There is no such thing as free anything, never mind drugs. I did however say yes, and that is where my life would change forever.

Needless to say they were all nice and accommodating, even when cooking up (preparing the heroin for injection). As soon as the gear hit my veins I knew deep in my heart and soul that I had royally fucked up. That is when, one by one they gang raped me for hours. One would hold my head and force me to sniff poppers (Alkyl Nitrate), when I started to fight back, when I had the strength they would just dose me up more and more.

I'm not a religious man, never have been, I hated the idea after having Catholic beliefs forced on me, but in my doped up haze I hoped and prayed to God that this would end and when it did it would never happen again.

But it did, for what felt like an eternity, although in reality it was just over 4 years I think. I say I think because I lost count of the days, I never knew the time, only day and night. I used to try to fight back, but in the end there was never any point, it would always end the same way, in rape by multiple men.

After a while, a year or so of what they called service, I would be allowed out of the room. To make my own food, to sit with them, smoke and drink tea with them.

I bloody hate tea!

This was only after I surrendered to the fact I was theirs. This was my job, my life now. Not that I owned my life, they did, I was just a product to be used and abused.

Oh how they did that.

It wasn't just the life I had to surrender to, it was the way I would be treated. I was a whore, a hole to be used as a sex toy by anyone who paid.

What is the worth of a man? £80 to £100 a time apparently.

The humiliation came in the form of being used as furniture. This meant being forced to kneel on the floor naked and to be used as a seat, as an ashtray, as a table and mainly as 2 holes to penetrate. Do you know how painful it is to have a cigarette put out on your skin? It's a pain you never get used to, no matter how hard you grit your teeth.

I spoke when I was spoken to, did as I was told and be the plaything of sadistic men twenty four seven.

I don't know why they let me go, why one day I was told to get dressed, taken out and driven into the countryside and left, but I was. Perhaps they grew bored, perhaps not. Maybe I was too old. I will never know.

How did they know I wouldn't go straight to the police?

One thing I never was, or will be, is a grass. Alright so you might think that I am a snitch for doing this, well that is up to you. I cannot change how you think or feel, but I will finish with this.

I got myself checked at the hospital not long after. I was found to have hepatitis A, B and C and HIV. I was very bitter and angry, anyone would be. It took me a long time to accept the unwanted gifts. I used to call them a curse, especially the latter. It was in those days that HIV was still a stigma, well it still is to be honest. It was seen as a death sentence. It isn't that anymore. Mine was caught before it was full blown AIDS and with the medical and pharmaceutical advancements over the years, I am undetectable and healthy, and as long as I keep solid with my medicine I will stay free for a long time and never advance to AIDS. Mind you, saying that, in my work, in a professional capacity, in a personal capacity and a community capacity as a church outreach worker I have met people who had full blown AIDS and on death's door who have had the effects reversed and are now living normal lives and are undetectable. Maybe one day we can irradiate this disease. I dedicate my life to inform and educate on the matter.

I tell you my story to educate.
I tell you my story to help future vulnerable runaways, so they don't make the same mistakes as I did.

I tell you my story because there are thousands, if not millions of young men and women trapped in sexual slavery.

I tell you my story freely because I know that neither I nor they will ever be identified. Not even the author of this book will ever know my real name or the full truths about my life.

I tell you my story so that those who are still bound to that life have hope in a future away from abuse and slavery.

I tell you my story so that anyone who had a hand in my abuse knows one thing - I forgive you because unforgiveness is poison to me. I love you because I am commanded to. I don't have to like you, trust you, see you, speak to you or think of you again. You have no power over me, but I do remember what you did so that my story can educate others.

I tell you my story as testimony of the freedom found in God - love. It does not matter whether you believe in Him or not, the fact is that He believes in you. That is the reason He died and the reason that I have been free for over 25 years physically and nearly 20 years spiritually and emotionally.

My whole life I believed in the lies that they told me, that I told myself. Remember these bare truths.

No matter who you are or what your situation, you are loved, wanted, respected, valued.

You are stronger than you think
Needed more than you will ever know irrespective of whether you believe it or not.

It is only through finding a faith in Jesus Christ, learning that I was broken and as much a slave to myself, to my own negativity and unforgiveness as much as I was to my abusers. God will never judge you and nor will I. May you find Him now.

....

Chapter Notes

Finn's story has really sat upon my heart for a while now. He was one of the few males I spoke to in relation to this book. I guess it sits with me, resounds with a familiarity with me in the fact that we grew up not too far apart in the same sort of timescale. His drug usage and fall came about when I would have been starting my own experimentation. I have no idea if we may have even crossed paths at a certain point as I did some debt collection in that area for a little while and came across several dealers in that area. I guess I will never know.

His voice was mainly upbeat as he used humor to mask his obvious pain. He came across as a little excitable and his tone would only drop a little when he was explaining something that gave him some obvious upset.

What kind of spirit, what kind of strength and resilience must a man have to be able to live through those events and speak so openly and honestly about them whilst remaining upbeat and humorous?

The Hidden

Jen

I worked the streets as a sex worker from the age of 18 to the age of 40. Not every sexual slave has a physical master, sometimes we are slaves to the situations we find ourselves in, to the lives we lead.

I am not going to tell you about my life, my situation or my past. My story is my own and I would like to keep it that way, at least for now. I had my reasons to become a sex worker and maybe one day I will tell my story in full, but for now my involvement in this project of Jack Gregory's remains one as more of a backseat role. As a contributor not by my story but by my thoughts, feelings and experience of the whole Sex industry. That being said I will proceed.

Through my whole career I have met a great many girls (some guys but not many to be honest) that have worked the many different aspects of the industry as a whole. Street workers, escorts, adult films, table top and lap dancing, modeling, the fetish scene etc. The whole industry has lots of layers from the so called tasteful to the downright seedy and frankly dangerous.

I once read that Prostitution is the oldest career and I can see why. As sex workers we are hidden in plain sight, there for one thing only, to please the men that pay for the services. I'm sure they have their reasons as to what we do when we work the industry. I have heard some real horrific stories from girls and punters alike.

Whilst the media still shows young girls unrealistic expectations of how they should look, whilst the fashion industry tells the young how they should dress, what make up to wear and tells them they need to look like the airbrushed celebrities on unrealistic and un-affordable diets, then things won't even begin to change.
Another factor to remember is that women as a whole are sexualised. This is mainly what the men want, what they like, what turns them on. I can't blame all of them either, they are told by the mass media what to like too. It's messed up.

Whilst we are seen as a sexualised stereotype, whilst pornography still exists, and whilst we are seen as marketable objects, then sex workers will always have a job to do and the mainstream industry will always hog the money and exploit them most. Attitudes need to change in every camp.

I can't really comment on the male sex work scene as I understandably have had no experience in that, which is why I am only talking about girls in general.

Where was I? Oh yeah, sorry I lost my train of thought for a moment or two.

Every girl who works the industry has a reason to do so, whether by choice, need, circumstance, whether willing or forced. We all have our crosses to bear. I also believe wholeheartedly that Street Work is the most dangerous of all.

It was only a few years ago when the Suffolk Strangler struck and every girl I know had to take extra precautions when working, some even quit altogether. Can't blame them really. It's a scary mad world out there and in my line of work at the time I had to stay as safe as I could and also keep my eye out on some of the other girls.

I have known girls forced into this life, with no means of escape, intimidated and fearful. Sold into sexual slavery. Some have stayed, knowing no other life. Some have escaped never to look back and some have died trying. It's heartbreaking, but what can girls who work the streets do but watch out for them. We cannot go to the police, we have no one we can really tell. The charity workers mean well but all we can really do is self preservation.

Personally, I left the streets several years ago but it does not mean I don't care about the next generation.

....

Chapter Notes

Just like Aiesha, Jen had the desire to have an input in this book but did not want to give too much of her own story away for one reason or another. She did however wish to add comparisons between her life and those who maybe still living it.

She had several points in mind that she wanted to get across. She came across well spoken and brought across the point that most of her education has come as an adult and desires to one day work in some form of social work or youth work. However, this would be outside of her home town as she made clear the point that to begin her emotional and spiritual recovery she needed to be as far away from home as possible.

She told me that although she now has a good relationship with her family; her home town is still an emotional place for her and causes too many bad memories, which in turn causes her a lot of distress.

Ten Years The Slave

Tredyk

For nearly 10 years I was a slave. For nearly 10 years I nearly broke my back daily just to pay off a debt, a debt that would increase daily, a debt that was not even my own, yet when asked if the decision I made would be different, the answer would be no.

The debt belonged to my brother. He was a worker, a foreman in Albania. I was barely 16 and he was 28. He was working in construction and he had an accident where he fell and broke his back. He was unable to work, he was unable to pay for equipment he had hired, and he was unable to pay back loans he had because if you are sick, if you have a day of, if you don't turn up then you do not get paid.

My family relied on his wages to live and because my brother could not pay, they took all of our stuff and we had nothing, yet they insisted we owed more. His debt is our debt. My brother could not walk again, never mind work again. The men when they came wanted to take my 11 year old sister to pay the debt, but I had heard so many bad stories about what these girls are made to do, how they are made to live, I could not allow my precious sister to go through that. My mother needed her and I love her, I love my brother and mother so I asked that they take me. I asked them how long it would take to pay the debt, how long I would be away from my family and they said it would be paid when it is paid. I would be free when they say.

I prepared myself for not seeing my family for a year or two; it would be nearly 10 years until I would see my sister. I did not realize that I would never see my mother or brother ever again. I sometimes wake up and cry with grief because I see their face in my dreams and remember the look on my mother's face. The tears that my sister cried and my brother once a hero, so fit and so strong then so fragile, so broken and unable to walk, bound to his bed trapped in his own body, a prisoner of his own mind. All of these images, these dreams break my heart every day.

I was taken away in a truck with other workers. This was late because it had already begun to get dark. We were taken to what was a farm and led into an outbuilding/barn. This would become my home for a while along with about 30 other people. There were a few women there, but they were older. Some had infant children with them. Many of us did not even have a blanket to keep warm at night, so we often would sleep huddled together so our bodies could heat each others.

We worked in the fields sometimes 16 hours a day with little food or water but what we did eat and drink we would be charged for, it would be added to the debt. I would try to go as long as I could without food so my debt would be gone quicker but I would get so weak and need to eat.

I used to think that dying would be easier, but I knew the debt would go to my family if I did and I could not bear this life for them. So in the end I worked, I ate and slept. I used to think it was hard on me, but you imagine being a 50, 60 or 70 year old woman with an infant tied to your back whilst you worked. Not only would you have to feed yourself, you would have to feed the little one. We would all save a little food for the children so they could have extra food and water. They needed to be taken care of, it was not their fault.

I also thought that all of these women were grandmothers to the infants, but I would find out later that this was not always true. Sometimes in the night some men would come drunk. They would take one or two of the women, I soon found out that the men would rape them.

Imagine that! Men of no older than 40 taking elderly women, the youngest being in her 50s, the oldest being in her 80s and raping them. To rape anyone is a disgusting act, but to do this to a woman that could be your grandmother makes you want to rage, to kill, but what could we do, we were weak, hungry and in debt, our families needed us.

We would try to take on some of the responsibilities for the care of the children so the women could rest more but work was hard and long and we needed to rest.

One of the female children had turned 6, (I now know her mother was nearly 70 years old) She was taken away, dragged from her mother's arms kicking and screaming, whilst her mother was inconsolable. I dare not imagine what happened to her for I fear my heart might break in grief.

After being there for several months, a few of the younger women like me were taken away in the truck. We would never see that farm again or the people, the family I had become used to. We would take care of each other, share the burden, share the weight of the work, share our food and not to mention our body heat on those cold nights.

The next place I was taken to was a little more livable if you can call it that. It was a room in a house that I shared with 5 other men. The house had 4 bedrooms with 6 men in each and a living room where 10 men would sleep at night and we would share in the time between work and sleep.

We were not allowed to leave the house except for work and when we were taken to different jobs. Our food was shared although the portions were bigger but again everything we had, the food in our stomach, the clothes on our back, the shoes on our feet, the equipment we used, the roof over our head well they were all classed as a loan with no written terms or conditions. The only conditions were that we worked and did as we were told.

We were taken to different places every day to work; even the transport was loaned to us. It was then that I knew that I would likely never be a free man.

On my 17th birthday my employers found out what day it was. They told me in the morning that if I do good at work today they say they have a present for me in the evening, that they give me a man's birthday because I am 17 and 17 is a man. I was worried because I did not know what would happen.

I worked hard all day (I did every day) on a construction site and was taken back to the house afterward. When they dropped me off the driver said "Boy we give you mans during tonight, we treat you like man, you will have good time". I do not need to tell you how nervous I was.

When the time came they come get me. This time I was taken in a car sat between 2 large men. They just looked at me, smiled at me and my heart was beating so fast I thought it may jump out of my chest. The journey must have taken 30 minutes or so. I was taken into an apartment; it was quite nice to look at. There were several men there all drinking alcohol, laughing. Something in the air did not feel right, I felt so uneasy.

After a while a big bald man with lots of tattoos handed me a drink, I did not want to take it but he had started to become a little aggressive and I did not want any trouble so I drank it. It was hot at the back of my throat and it made me cough. They all laughed at me.

I was made to sniff cocaine. Again I did not want to but I did not want trouble. I did not feel well at all.

I was not there a long time before I was taken to a bedroom where at least 10 men sat around the edges. On the bed was one of the older ladies from the farm. She was maybe 65 years old. She was naked and I felt embarrassed, the only other body I had ever seen naked apart from my own was that of my little sister when I helped to bathe her.

One of the men spoke. "Boy take off your clothes, tonight you become a man". I did not want to and I shake my head and say no but one man puts a large knife to her throat and said he would slit her throat if I did not, so under that pressure I took off my clothes so I was also naked.

Please forgive me if I do not go into too much further detail. I do not wish to either offend or shock, although I realize that you may already be a little upset and disturbed by my story so far, for that I deeply apologize, I have been asked to share my story, to be as open and as honest as I feel comfortable with, so this is what I am doing.

All I will say about what happened next is that they made me watch them have sex with her and then I was forced to have sexual relations with her whilst they watched. I was a virgin at the time and very scared. When I looked at her she smiled with sadness hidden behind it. I knew this look so

I know she knew that I was trapped too, and with that in mind I will say no more about that if you do not mind.

After the whole thing they make me drink more, sniff more cocaine and they would take me back to the house at sunrise. I was only allowed to get a clean up, I had no sleep and still felt ill from the drugs they made me take.

On site I told them I did not feel good, they just laughed and told me to get to work. During that day I fell into some bricks and broke my left arm. I could not tell them what I had done, I had to carry on the best I could and strap my arm up when I got back to the house. One of the other men in my room looked at it. He said it was broken and dislocated. I had to bite on a wooden spoon as it was put back into place.

A few months later, after working and not long back at the house, some of the men from that night came and dragged me outside. They told me that the lady was pregnant and that it is me that is responsible for her.

They beat me hard, broke my nose and told me that I am now working for three as she cannot work whilst pregnant and that I have to feed a baby. They told me that my debt was so high it will never be paid in full. Up until that time I had kept a little hope of freedom, maybe I was naïve but I was still so young. It was then I gave in to the fact that I would probably never see my family again.

Back in my room the other men tell me that this is not the first time the men do this. I am told they do it to the young to keep them working for them. They tell me she is most likely without child and that I should forget even if she was with child because I would never see it. I could not forget though, the poor woman and poor child. It would be fatherless and I knew what that is like.

I would ask to see her every day but they just push me away and laugh, tell me to go back to work, but I keep asking anyway, if she have a boy or girl. They do not tell me.

After working maybe 2 more years I was working on a farm and a boy from where I grew up is there. He is maybe 2 or 3 years younger than me.

He told me that my brother had died and not long after my mother who also died. My heart was broken; I had really lost all hope. I ask what happened to my sister and I was told she run away. The last he knew she was safe. I did not believe in any sort of God. I would think if he exists then why would he allow this suffering, but I prayed to who or whatever that she would be safe. I hoped, I so much wanted her to be safe, to be free.

Do you know I would dream of her every night. She would be grown and having escaped she would have found a family that would take her in, a kind family, a loving family with enough money to give her education. She would learn in the best schools, she would grow to become a lawyer. She would marry for love like my mother did and have beautiful children overseas. She would live a long and wonderful life and so would her husband. Our father had died when she was only young leaving my mother with 3 children to feed, but her children would know the love of a father until they were old. One day we would find each other and we would be family again with me and my child.

Do you think that is a strange thing to think, to believe? Did I just fool myself? Whatever the answer I did not care. That hope, that dream was the only thing that was left to keep me going, to make me not want to die, to not kill myself. I didn't even know if I would be better off dead because in my mind the debt was paid but they would never let me be free.

So what could I do but work, and work to my best. Although I had broken my arm in the accident and had some ongoing weakness, I was still strong and good at my work. They would move me back and forth between the construction sites and the farms. I would hope and pray to see her, to see my child, I never did. I don't know what hurts the most, having a child and not being able to see it or not knowing if you have a child but long to know. Either way it hurts your heart.

I keep working hard, do as I am told and always polite. I guess I had been there for years, I did not know if I would ever see my freedom but it would soon come.

By this time I now held some trust with them, I knew no other life really. I would take on the new boy at the farm and on the sites to show them what to do. People would come and go from the accommodation, the old would die and we would get new people. I guess the time I had been there maybe half of the people who I lived with from the start were still there.

One day on the construction site there was an accident. One of the older workers he had a heart attack I guess and he fell. The men they panicked whilst I sit there and comfort him as he lay dying. I just hold his hand. Tell him it will be OK, that he will be OK. I wanted to cry but could not, I would cry for him in private.

The men they say to get him in the car, to sit with him, they know he die soon. I thought they may have humanity and take him to a doctor but they just drive to the middle of nowhere and drop him in a ditch. I could see the death waiting upon his face. He give his life, his strength and they throw him away like trash.

It was in the room that evening that the idea came to me. I know if it goes wrong they will kill me, but at that moment I realize that the only freedom will come through death or success. I want to live but I had decided not to care if I live or die, I would rather that than this life anymore. I know the men they are not stupid, but I know they cannot, will not carry the week and sick. It cost them too much money. I know this from day 1 when my brother have his accident. They just leave him at the side of the road to die, but he was strong so he used his arms and hands to pull himself 9 miles home. I know that I would need to be hurt like this or worse, I would need to be that close to death or closer and I would need to find the strength to pull myself back, to fight or die.

The opportunity would soon come. I was working on the roof of the accommodation, there had been a leak. I can see the roof it is wet and slippy and that is the moment I close my eyes. I see the faces of my mother, my brother, my sister even my father. I knew, I decided, I chose to fall, and I did.

I did not feel pain, only numbness. I could see very little, only a mix of blurred vision and darkness. I could hear lots of voices, the panic but I could not hear it well because it sounded as if my head was under water. I remember being put into a car as I could feel the motion. The pain by now was so bad but I could not scream, I had to keep quiet and calm, so I bit down on my tongue.

I remember the pain as I hit the floor as they throw me from the car, I also hear a voice say "it is a shame, he was good worker".

I don't know how long I waited after they left, but it was getting dark when I opened my eyes.

My left shoulder was dislocated, my left hip broken, the bone in my left shin had come through my skin. My right foot was also broken and my knee hurt badly. I could not breath very well, it felt like I had a fat man sitting on my chest. When I do breath I can hear a rattle and I cough up blood. I will not lie, I thought about just giving up, laying there and dying but I see my sister in my mind and I find my strength and crawl on my right side and the pain got worse but I keep going.

I think I must have lost some time because I remember darkness. When I awake I am in a bed. I did not know where and I think they come back for me. I had been found by an old man who lived miles away from anybody. He tell me it is fine, I am going to be safe. He tended to my wounds, to my pain and bring me back to health. All this time in the back of my mind I think the men come for me, but they do not. It took a long time to heal my body and my mind may never heal fully.

I am afraid this is where I must finish, I cannot go into any more detail of how I would finally get away from Albania or who helped me. I will say that I still look over my shoulder and am as careful as I can be. Oh I did find my sister eventually but this is her story to tell.

was so bad but I could not scream, I had to keep quiet and calm, so I bit down on my tongue.

I remember the pain as I hit the floor as they throw me from the car, I also hear a voice say "it is a shame, he was good worker".

I don't know how long I waited after they left, but it was getting dark when I opened my eyes.

My left shoulder was dislocated, my left hip broken, the bone in my left shin had come through my skin. My right foot was also broken and my knee hurt badly. I could not breath very well, it felt like I had a fat man sitting on my chest. When I do breath I can hear a rattle and I cough up blood. I will not lie, I thought about just giving up, laying there and dying but I see my sister in my mind and I find my strength and crawl on my right side and the pain got worse but I keep going.

I think I must have lost some time because I remember darkness. When I awake I am in a bed. I did not know where and I think they come back for me. I had been found by an old man who lived miles away from anybody. He tell me it is fine, I am going to be safe. He tended to my wounds, to my pain and bring me back to health. All this time in the back of my mind I think the men come for me, but they do not. It took a long time to heal my body and my mind may never heal fully.

I am afraid this is where I must finish, I cannot go into any more detail of how I would finally get away from Albania or who helped me. I will say that I still look over my shoulder and am as careful as I can be. Oh I did find my sister eventually but this is her story to tell.

Gay Pari

Henri

Pari, Gay Pari, the city of romance and a tourists' dream. Boat rides on the river and young couples in love. Love in the air, locks on a bridge that signifies romance. I have a lock on this bridge, though it does not signify love, it signifies the bondage I lived, the pain I suffered and how hard it is to open once the keys are thrown in the river.

This city, a city that many people think is beautiful, this city wears a mask, it is a facade, a lie. Pari is an illusion created by hopeless romantics and bohemian art lovers. Once you get past the illusion, the mask, you can see the cracks, the dirt and once you get out of the main centre, you can smell the raw sewers and shite. For me Pari is a bitter and dirty place that kills love, not breeds it. I will never set a foot back into that place in eternity.

I apologise, I must sound so bitter and twisted No!

I shall carry on....
I knew I was different from a very young age. Don't get me wrong, I love being a man and liked being a boy but I did have an affinity for the female of the species. When my mamma could not see, I would sneak away and wear my sister's clothes. I was not born into the wrong body, I was in the right body, I just like feminine things. Sometimes I liked being mama's handsome boy but at times I just wanted to feel as pretty as my sister.

I kept it hidden for many years until I was caught by my papa. My papa was how you say, a man of men. Sorry a man's man. I was 17 and there was no one home. I had done this many times, wear my mother's clothes and make up. The truth is that I have never been masculine looking and once I had learned how to do my makeup I was very passable as a female. I have no idea why he came home but I did not hear him and he found me standing in front of my mama's full length mirror. He lost his temper and began to beat me all around the house.

When mama got home she cried, so hard I could not bear to see it, so I ran to my room, packed what I could and left, my papa spat at me as I went through the door, my mama could not look at me. Little did I know that this would be the last time I would see my mama in 5 years and until this day my papa refuses to see me, but that is a story for another time.

I emptied my savings from my bank account, I had maybe enough money for a week in a cheap hotel room and a little for food, but for now I know that I can be free to dress how I like in a place where nobody knew me. I took a little comfort in that, I also knew that at that time Paris had around 140 Gay bars so I know I can find somewhere to fit in.

Life is hard enough for a teenager, never mind a Homeless Gay, Cross Dressing teenager that has just lost his entire family. Needless to say, I was at the end of my world.

It was not long before I found a room that factoring in for food and other necessities I could afford, a roof over my head for maybe 2.5 weeks. I cannot describe how dirty the hotel was. It had an odour of stale cigarettes, cheap alcohol and wet laundry, but I could not complain, it was a roof over my head and protection.

For the first few nights I kept to myself, only leaving the room if I needed too. In the room I would spend my time reading. I would often sit around dressed as I felt comfortable, this often meant in feminine clothes and make up. For the first time I felt free to dress how I wanted, when I wanted.

I soon realized that the room next door was used mostly by prostitutes who needed to keep their business away from the streets, although they often found their customers there. There were maybe 5 or 6 different girls who worked from there. Over time I would get to know them all.

Out of all the girls in that room there was one who I would begin to talk to. I will keep her nameless but she was an older, larger lady with gray hair tied in a bun.

It was maybe 2 or 3 am and the alcoholic in the room across had managed to set his bed on fire, I presume he had fallen asleep in a drunken state. The fire alarms went off and the hallway outside was filled with smoke. I had fallen asleep reading and I was in full dress with makeup. I was woken with banging on the door and the sound of panic outside. I did not even think and went running outside. I only realized when some of the other occupants began to stare. The old lady didn't even turn her gaze when she stood next to me, I was scared, in panic and conscious of people looking at me. She put her hand on my shoulder and told me to ignore it. "Some people are afraid of what is different, they think you are different, you are not you are beautiful" she said. This made me smile, I felt like she had accepted me. When we were allowed back into our rooms she invited me for a drink and I accepted.

We spoke for the rest of the night and she seemed very kind and understanding. I told her of my life and the events that led me here. She told me she understood what it was like to feel different. She told me I was welcome there in whatever dress I felt like. I told her I did not have much money left, that I did not know what I was going to do, where I was going to go after it ran out. She told me about men who may pay to see me dressed like this, men who would treat me like a woman but desired more than a woman could offer. These men would pay for time with me, for sex with me or for me to have sex with them. I told her I was not sure, that I had only ever been with 2 men in my life but they had been a secret.

"You have a good body, feminine and look female. If I didn't mind sex then why not make a little money from the gift that God gave me. Sex is a natural thing so why not use it to pay for the room, food and more" She said.

I really wasn't sure, but I did not know what I was going to do, how I would even eat. She told me she would introduce me to her friend who could help. She would pay for my room for a few more days, I did not have to pay back. It sounded too good to be true and I would soon find out it was and that nothing in this life comes for free. As I said, I did not know how I was going to live so I eventually agreed. She told me to be at the hotel at 4 o' clock and she would tell me more. I nodded and smiled.

I must have paced my room for more than an hour waiting for the time to come. I was so focused on the pacing I nearly jumped out of my skin when she knocked on the door. She was not alone as I thought, she had a younger woman with her, a lady I recognized as one of the girls from the room.

They had bags and cases with them, I was confused by this. The old lady told me they were going to make me more beautiful, more stunning and sexy. She told me that I looked more like a woman than ever, that I had to look my best for him, he demanded the best.

The whole process must have taken hours. The younger one showed me how to bind my penis so I would look more like a woman in underwear. They gave me a real hair wig glued on to my actual hair, and helped me shave all over my body. They gave me everything from beautiful underwear to full make up, including breasts. I must admit when I saw myself in the mirror I was shocked. I could have believed it was really a woman looking back at me had it not been me standing there.

For the first time in my life I felt closer to a woman that I ever had. They say I am still Henri and I can be him when I like, they say I need a feminine name for when I wanted to feel female, to be female. I always liked the name Zarah, so we decided on this and it turned out that I would be known as her more than I would be known as myself. Little did I know that this would be one of the last times that I would be Henri in around 5 years.

We sat in the room next door for a while we waited for him. They told me his name was Ettiene and that he will love me, I just have to do as I am told, be polite and he will treat me nice.

Ettiene was an older, very handsome man with brushed back brown hair. He was muscular and very masculine. He smiled at me when he walked in. He wore a fitted grey suit and held himself very businesslike. I was very attracted to him and he could see that and would use it to his advantage. He came across very kind and generous, he made me a drink, he was funny and charming and made me feel at ease. I had never met a man like him before, he seemed to accept me as I was. He then asked the others to leave and we made love. When we had finished he told me he wanted to take care of me because he takes care of his friends. He gave me money and said he would come and see me again in a few days and he would like to take me for a meal and a night out.

Thinking back on it now, I can see how naïve I really was but I just wanted to be wanted, accepted and loved for the way I was, for the way I felt and in all of my life these were the only people who showed me any sort of kindness and acceptance.

He took me to a really beautiful bistro and he told me he could help me earn money being Zarah. He told me that there are men who would like to be with me as Zarah, that I would have sex with them for money. He told me that sex with other men did not mean anything, that what we had together was special and we would be in a relationship, he would be my boyfriend and it is not sex between us, it is making love. I liked the sound of that. I liked him a lot and what we had together felt special, he made me feel special. He told me when I am with other men all I need do is close my eyes and think of him. He told me that sex would be my job but making love with him would be a pleasure and with that I agreed.

Over the next few weeks things went ok. He would send me gifts, send me flowers and be next door when the customers would come. I was nervous at first but after the men left he would come to see me, hold me and tell me I had done well. Then he took me there, to that party and my life would change forever.

It was in a beautiful house about an hour outside Pari. I was dressed in a beautiful evening gown and the best black lingerie. All of the men there were dressed in high end suits and there were 2 women who were all like me, not real women at all but very convincing. I had never met anyone like me but they were different. They would act one way around the men and different around each other. One of them told me to have a drink, that it would help me with what is about to come.

This confused me, it would not confuse me for long. I would see the truth soon enough. Ettienne came over and kissed me, he told me that this would be the last time in a while that I would have to be with any other man but him. He told me we would go away somewhere to the south for a few days and he would spoil me.

In my mind I thought that I would have to have sex with maybe 2 or 3 men. I was at a point in my life where the attention, the love from Ettienne was what I thought that I needed. I loved him, I would have done anything for him. I did do anything for him, everything and anything he asked, but this made me feel uneasy and I told him so.

His face changed and his eyes burned into me. I had only ever seen that look upon my father's face. Despite that he remained composed and took a deep breath, he put his hands upon my shoulders, this he had done before but his hands felt heavy and tight.

"I love you, I would never hurt you, you know this" he said.
"But there is no choice, we have been paid, do not embarrass me. Do I not always treat you with kindness" he followed.

I was scared, all I could do was nod. He kissed me on my lips and led me into a side room. In the room there was only a bed. He sat there with me for a few moments then pushed me down and tied my wrists with restraints to the top corners of the bed. He told me to relax, I did not like this, I did not want to do this but I had no choice. I thought he was getting up to leave but he walked to the end of the bed and pushed my legs up to my shoulders and bound them to my wrists and then he left without saying a word.

I will not describe what followed in great detail, I do not wish to be crass or pornographic in my words, but you have to understand the situation I found myself in. I was gagged with a ball, I was raped by 25 men that night, they hurt me, slap me, humiliate me. They spit on me and insert things inside me and when it was all over I could not walk, all I could do was cry. I felt so sick, so dirty, so used and like I was not a human. I had just been used as a sex doll by 2 dozen men. I just wanted to die.

I was told I was not allowed to even shower until I got home. I hurt so much I could not even sit. I just lay on the back seat of the car sobbing and unable to get out a single audible word whilst Ettienne drove. He was silent, he would not say a word. I looked out of the window and did not know where we were. I did not recognize the streets, the roads, this was not Pari.

I mustered up the strength to ask where we were, where we were going. "I told you, I am taking you away". His voice was different, more stern, more serious. I did not want to push him to find out how angry he would get so I just submitted to the fact and lay on the back seat and try to control the pain.

I guess I must have passed out from the pain because by the time we arrived, it had started to get dark again. My whole ordeal had lasted all night and we left early in the morning sometime after 9 am. It was a small country chateau with nothing but fields surrounding it.

Ettienne had started being nice again, he even helped me out of the car and took me straight into a small bedroom and then helped me onto the bed. The pain was so bad that no position that I tried helped. The only position that gave me the least amount of pain was on my side with my knees curled into my stomach. The bedroom had a small en suite bathroom. He went and ran me a bath and gave me pain killers swilled down with wine.

He told me he was sorry for what I had been through, that it was too much. He said that he thought it was all a bit of fun that had gotten out of hand. He led me to the bath, undressed me and helped me in and then left.

He came back around 30 minutes later I guess. He held an almost empty bottle of red wine that he had been drinking straight from the bottle. He was quite drunk and slurred his words as he stumbled towards me, he seemed quite happy and loving. He began to wash me, to touch me and kiss me, this got me angry after the ordeal I had suffered. I tried to brush it off, to push him away but he kept on, he was much stronger than me.

He told me he loved me but I did not love him. He told me if I loved him I would not be like this. I told him no, I was in pain and he got angry. He pulled me out of the bath by my hair. He slapped me, hit me, kicked me. He told me that this is my fault, he loves me but I need to be taught a lesson. He told me he does not like doing this because it hurts him more than me. He then raped hard me right there on the bathroom floor and when he finished he just walked away laughing whilst I lay there crying.

For a week or two things would go quiet. He would allow me to recover, he would give me pain relief always followed by wine. He would leave the chateau to get supplies, he would always lock me in. When he got home he would drink wine until he would fall asleep.

The pain had mostly subsided and at least I was able to walk better, albeit with a limp. I waddled around like a constipated penguin.

Please do not think that I am making light of the situation with that remark, nothing could be further from the truth. As a person, as a survivor I have to find away to cope and humour is one of those ways, I mean nothing by it, it is only a way for me to be able to gain courage to carry on.

Ettienne had become a man so very different from the one I met all those months ago. He had become my captor, my jailer and my only crime was being me. I had pretty much submitted to the fact that I had lost him and I was comfortable with that. I had decided that I'd had enough of the pain of rape, so I made the decision to just let him do what he wanted to, get it over as quickly as possible, even pretend to enjoy it just to get it over quicker.

He was drinking so much, he was no longer the man I met. By this time I was no longer Zarah, I was not even dressing as her. I was Henri and for the first time in my life I was strangely comfortable with that.

"Zarah is dead, long live Henri".

I knew his routine, how to control him and I had decided to make my escape.

Once he returned from the supply run I served him a bottle of his wine and waited until he started to become drunk. I took care of him sexually because I knew he would fall asleep after, and once he slept no amount of noise would awaken him.

As he slept I took the key from around his neck and the car keys from his pocket and emptied his wallet of 500 francs and let myself out and locked him in. I surprised myself with the courage I had found.

I knew he wouldn't awaken but I did not want to take a chance so I pushed the car a little way down the lane. I had never driven a car before but I had watched Ettienne and was a pretty quick learner. After stalling a few times I managed to drive away. I kept to the back roads, staying away from the main track. I eventually left the car in a ditch and made my way to the closest railway station.

I did not know where I was going to go but I knew I could not go back to Pari . I paid when I needed to, stowed away when I could. From the very moment I escaped from him I decided I would never, should never look back. For a few years I worked where I could to earn enough money to get me by. When and where I could not find work I would sell myself, usually in the back streets, truck stops and public restrooms.

I mostly stayed off the radar but I wanted a passport so I found a short term apartment and a job in a small town. I kept myself to myself until I got what I needed.

I eventually found myself in Holland and that is where I stayed for many years and built up my life, but that is another story for another time.

Chapter Notes

I managed to speak to Henri on several occasions via telephone so I have no real reference to what he looks like or even how old he is. He was always softly spoken and his grasp of English was very good. On a few occasions he struggled to find the right word or phrases but he was mostly well spoken and quite articulate.

One of the things that stood out for me was the humor he used to cope, some on the verge of crude so there are a few bits that I have left out in the edit. He told me that humor is his first response to pain.

There were several times in the interviews where his voice would break and genuine distress would rear its head. When asked if he wanted to stop the interview he would compose himself and carry on.

Reset the Default

Sandra

There are so many lies that we tell ourselves to survive our relative short time upon this earth.

I am not good enough, I can't, I am weak, I am ugly, no one would love a person like me, the list goes on and we are caught up in an infinite cycle of self destruction and that BIG RED BUTTON, that trigger can take only one word to set it off and then it's hell to pay.

My whole life I believed the lies, the lies told by others, the ones I told myself and at several points in my life total self destruction ensued leaving a wake of grief and pain. The biggest lie for me was

"I am worthless, but my body isn't".

For me it began at home, a place our hearts are supposed to be, where the warmth of the family keeps it beating. My heart did not beat to the tune of love, it beat to the rhythm of fear, of loathing, of hate. Words used like bricks, the weapon of choice to cause maximum damage from a distance. Whereas a brick may break a window, a wrongly used word can shatter your soul. Yet we keep going back out of the fear of loss, who wants to lose their family? Blood is blood, right?

It starts with those little digs, those throwaway comments masked as humor. Those comments about weight, those comments about being silly, don't be daft, you know I don't mean it, only joking and the list goes on and on and on. Every little comment taken to heart and we begin to believe them.

This for my life, well the most of it anyway has been my default setting. A misplaced word, a throwaway comment and there I was offended, but I did not say anything, I would never, could never say anything because I would fear offending the people I thought I loved. Fighting for attention and I would keep my pain to myself, in fear.

My mother wouldn't say anything when my father would come in drunk, she too lived in fear of his poisoned tongue, his violent temper, childlike tantrums and his all too common frenzied fists. She took it, his temper, his rage. All too many times she would have a bruise, a black eye and blame it on her clumsy nature, blame it on herself. We knew it was not her, we could hear the commotion in the night, we would rarely see him hit her, we would just see the damage, on the occasions we did, then she would just tell us she deserved it, it was her fault, and at most in our infancy we believed it.

As volatile as my home life was school could be much worse. As important as education is we rarely see the point in our younger lives. We would compare the stricter teachers to Hitler and we would try to manipulate the softer ones for our own personal benefit. History, math, English and art are not the only subjects we learn at school. Manipulation is learned, mostly on the playground.

The school system is full of cliques, the cool kids, the sporting kids, the intelligent, the naughty, the attractive, the ugly....you get my drift? and this cliques begin on day 1.

I was always on the outside. I was the overweight weird girl from the poor family. Everything I owned from my uniform, my clothes, my shoes and even my pens and pencils were hand me downs. My hair was kept short to keep the nits at bay because school was an infinite breeding ground for head lice and because I was the poor fat kid with short hair and hand me down uniform I often got the blame for the infestations of itch heads and the cause of the rise of crew cuts for the boys in my school. Oh yes and I neglected to mention that this was only early middle school.

Most of the kids were shipped off to the same high school in the same town, so that label I was given on day 1 stuck.

I had very little interest in boys and by the time I moved up I had become tired of the jokes, the comments, the blatant bullying so I attempted to adapt and be the weird kid, the goth, in hope that I might be weird enough to be left alone, at least to my face. After all if it was behind my back I could ignore it, the fact is that it just got gradually worse, because of this not only was I fat and poor I was the fat smelly lesbian.

I would contemplate suicide, I hated my life and everything about it. I just wanted to talk to someone but I feared that I would not be taken seriously, after all who would take the suicidal goth kid seriously.

Home was getting worse, mum was an emotional wreck most of the time. Smoking and drinking just to get by.

The first time my father abused me physically was confusing to me to say the least. He had come home in an unusually good mood. He had won several hundred pounds on the dogs. He had had a few to drink but wasn't yet in his unusual inebriated state. I guess I was around 13 years old. I was slightly overweight, my breasts were fully grown and I had pretty much gotten everything physically that puberty had to offer.

It was a Saturday, There was nobody home as mum was out shopping with my younger siblings as she always did on a Saturday.
I had been in the bath and was laying on my bed in just my towel listening to a mix tape on the hand me down Walkman I had gotten the previous Christmas.

Dad came bounding in and sat on the end of my bed giggling to himself. He handed me a small package and told me that he had won on the dogs and bought me a present. It was a small silver crucifix on a chain. It was quite pretty and I liked it so I smiled. He told me that he did love me, that he didn't always mean the bad things he said to me. He told me that no matter what anyone said that I was a beautiful young woman. He stroked my face, this was the first time I had seen him so tactile and loving. I was actually happy.

"Give your old man a kiss" he said.

He even turned his cheek so I went to give him one and as I did he turned his face to mine and gave me a violent kiss. The force was so much that I fell back on the bed and he used that to his advantage. He clambered on top of me. I tried to push him off but he was too strong. His mouth still forced against mine. When he did remove his mouth I could barely breath never mind scream.

I always thought my dad could be a monster when he had been drinking but I never in my life thought he would sink this low. He covered my mouth with his left hand baring all of his weight on me so I could not move and proceeded to rape me. Physically it probably lasted a matter of a few minutes but mentally….well I still live it.
I relive everything that anyone has ever done to me on a daily basis. Yes I cope, mostly because of my child but I can never forget, especially the first time.

When he had finished he stumbled away just smirking and I was left in tears knowing that I could never tell, no one would ever believe me.

I ran in to the bathroom, bolted the door and fell to the floor truly broken. I must have scrubbed myself for over an hour, I couldn't get clean.

The rapes continued for around a year when the old bastard finally died of a massive heart attack. Is it wrong to have laughed when it happened? I would never be free from what he did, ever.
School was getting worse, the bullying, the names.
It was around this time that I was introduced to the local pharmacist if you know what I mean. My father's death had left my mother in so much debt that we could barely afford to eat never mind anything else. John would let me eat there, he would always feed me and give me drugs, all I had to do in return was give him sexual favors. After all, what did sex matter after I had been repeatedly raped by a man who was supposed to have loved me. Why not use my body for my own gain? I rarely had money but I always had a body. Remember that I was only around 14 years old at this time.

The rumors started around school and the boys who bullied me were the boys with cash in their pocket and a cock in their hand. Who was I to say no?

At 18 I left home, nowhere to go but to stay with my pharmacist. As always rent was paid in sexual favours for his spare bedroom. As soon as I moved in I had already pretty much decided that I would be selling my body for cash, why not? Pay my rent and make some money and that is what I did for 20 years.

John would sit downstairs and listen for trouble. Incidentally I married John and we were together until he died very recently. He would take care of me. I guess I did love him in my own way.

Throughout the years I have been asked to do so many degrading things, and I did because I knew very little else. I won't go into what I did, but needless to say even Hugh Hefner would blush.

You see my default setting was to appear not to care, to believe that I was not good enough, not beautiful, not wanted, not worth anything except as a sexual aid. My default setting also was self destruction and the whole storm that follows. My default setting was to put everyone in the same box, distrust and self preservation.
It is only through working on myself, my own thought processes that I have been able to find that little girl inside and begin my life again.

My father may have been responsible for the destruction of my innocence, but I was and still am responsible for the way I lived and the choices that I made. I chose to tell no one, through fear, I greatly admire those who have had the courage to stand up and be counted. I was responsible for the chemicals I put into my body. I was responsible for using my own body for the pleasure of others, these are the choices I made and it took me a long time to learn to live with them.

For so many years I blamed others, blamed everyone, anyone else for my own problems.

Through faith, in a God of my own understanding, through the 12 step programs of Alcoholics and Narcotics Anonymous, through self development and therapy, I have learned to reset my thought processes and default settings and learned to customize my own proverbial desktop.

I learned to love myself, that way it does not matter what others think. I learned to live with myself and trust my own judgment, after all how am I expected to trust anyone else if I do not trust myself.

When there are problems I take it to God first then those I trust.

Most of my life has been fight or flight, now it's Surrender to Win. This does not mean I give up, Surrender means to surrender to the will of God as we understand him, to that higher power. There are things we can change and things we can't. It does not matter what situation it can be dealt with using 1 simple prayer that can be used in any situation.

God

Grant me the serenity to accept the things that I cannot change, the courage to change the things I can and the Wisdom to know the difference

....

Chapter Notes

I was introduced to Sandra by a friend from the local Christian Network. We only had a relatively short time together so the conversation was kept to a tight schedule. We met up at the Virgin Money Lounge in Norwich.

Before we met I advised our mutual friend to ask her to bring a friend. I was told that she kept her circle of friends tight so it would be him that came with her.

We only had an hour to complete the interview and it was requested that I write my notes and not record them as I would usually do. This was one of the interviews that I just sat and listened. She was a stern sounding woman who never really broke tone. The whole thing was formal which is something I am not used to, most other interviews I have conducted have been on a more informal, friendly basis.

A Letter to My Mother

Dear Mom

I LOVE YOU

Because despite everything you have ever done you gave birth to a good man.

Oh and Mom I HATE YOU for all you put me through in the world you made me live in, your world.

Mom I CRY FOR YOU for the bond between mother and son is supposed to be so strong, an unbreakable bond of unconditional love. A babe is supposed to suckle at its mothers breast not lay in a broken basket and gaze upon a man with his face where mine should be, for sustenance not sexual gratification.

A child should grow and wander about his home not be left in the living room to watch the television whilst he wonders what the noises are coming from the room next door. Should a child not be able to walk from room to room without the worry of stepping over dirty needles and used condoms, discarded without care, a bit like me really.

Should a child not have its innocence for as long as possible instead of losing it the second it was born.

Should it not have been you tucking me into bed instead of a random man or even me covering you with a dirty blanket when you lay unconscious on the sofa as naked as the day you were born, yet how could I watch you shake in the cold. Should it not be mother caring for son and not the other way around.

Should a child not fall asleep to a lullaby and not loud inaudible music mixed with the voices of too many random people laughing, shouting and

84

drinking from the foul smelling glass bottles. Staggering and vomiting upon my toy box.

Should a child not be able to sleep without the fear of one of the many men you make me call uncle calling in the night and touching me in the personal places that I have barley learned the names for.

Oh and mom how can you hold my hand whilst he touches me, kisses me. How can you tell me that you love me and let me go through that, and how can you let it happen so many times, by so many men.

Even though you put me through all of this, Mom I STILL LOVE YOU because you taught me how not to be, how not to act and to treat everyone with love because I could never bare to treat my children the way you taught me.

Mom, I HATE YOU for the person that you were, for making me hate you the way I do, but Mom I LOVE YOU, because I am commanded to.

Mom, I forgive you because if I don't I may poison my own life and you have caused me enough pain and suffering.

NO MORE!

In forgiveness I REJECT YOU, your ways and everything that you were.

Mom I PRAY FOR YOU, even though you are no longer here because I know you made a deal with Satan long ago, you may never be judged upon this earth by its law but you will be judged by Him.
Mom, with this letter I LET YOU GO, there is no longer any room in my life for you.
So Mom I say GOODBYE because your circumstance is the direct consequence of your life, your actions and my life is better without you.

GOODBYE MOM

I LOVE YOU, I HATE YOU, I FORGIVE YOU

Your Son

Anon

Chapter Notes

This heartbreaking letter was sent to me to use in the book with the strict instruction that it be signed 'Anon'.

I cried for hours after receiving this and those words I love you, I hate you sit heavily upon my heart.

Unforgiveness has been a large part of my life and despite how poisonous it is I know how difficult it is to let go and have nothing but admiration and love for this man.

My journey has been a long one but I cannot help but feel that Anon's has been so much longer and harder.

Working Mother

Jake

My story is most likely a little different to the others in this book. The fact is that I was not abused as a child, I have not suffered sexual assault or rape and I don't believe that I have been exploited in any way whatsoever. I hold no qualifications whatsoever so I cannot really comment about exploitation from an educational view. What I can do is tell you about a woman I know well.

This woman is my rock, my best friend, my world but it was not always this way. I suppose this isn't really my story to tell it's hers. However, a lot of her story we share so I guess seeing some of the exploitation she went through qualifies me to speak about it. To tell you about her however I do need to tell you a little about me, and I am not always comfortable with doing that so here goes.

My mum was always a working girl in every sense. She met my father whilst working in a brothel. My dad was not a customer though, he was what you might call security for the girls. He would make his presence known when the customers came and then hang about in another room until an alarm was set off and also escort the men out of the door.

The way my mum tells it is that they had a connection to start with then quickly fell in love. They both decided that mum would stay working, truth be told she didn't want to stop, prostitution is all she knew. She had been in that line of work from 19 years old and she was 30 when she had me. They left the brothel to set up their own in another town. They had not long set up when dad was sent to prison for beating a customer half to death after he got rough with my mother. She was unknowingly in the early stages of pregnancy with me.

With my dad in prison on a 4 year sentence and no other form of income my mum needed to carry on working for as long as possible.

As she was working from a 4 bedroom rented house she brought in other girls to help supplement the income and rent until she could work again. She even worked whilst heavily pregnant with me, she told me that there were men who would pay heavily for sex with pregnant women.

I grew up around that life, my father in and out of prison for violence and when he wasn't he would sleep around with lots of different women. It's the only life I knew. I would sit and watch films with one of the girls whilst my mother worked. I never wanted or needed for anything, I guess you could say I was a little spoilt.

When I was 15 a customer robbed the girls in the house and there was nothing physically I could do. I wanted to protect her, to protect the other girls so I took up boxing and martial arts and became pretty good.

I would do the job my father used to do and it was ok for a while but the thing is my mum could get through a lot of men in a day. It got to the point when I couldn't stand seeing it anymore.

I wanted to kill each and every dirty bastard who touched her, so at 18 I got a job working the nightclub doors and got myself a small flat. I guess it was down to my own insecurities that I stopped talking to her, stopped seeing her and withdrew into my own self. Being a doorman at that time I had pretty much unlimited access to almost any drug I desired and cocaine became my crutch.

My life was falling apart. I had always thought I was a strong man but obviously my life affected me in a profound way, I guess that is why I kept my mother at a distance. I was falling deeper and deeper and about to hit rock bottom.
I had been suspended from work a couple of times through police investigations for being too heavy handed with nightclub clientele. I had only been back a few days and I was with a colleague and we were doing a sweep of the club. We got to the back of the club and the fire doors were ajar. When we got outside I found my mum with a punter and totally lost my rag, I must have blacked out in a rage and remember very little, only getting dragged off by several colleagues. The result was I put him in

intensive care for a month and physiotherapy for the rest of his life. I'm not proud of it.

My mum refused to speak to me for years. On the inside I completed several anger management classes and courses.

I found Jesus in my prison cell after completing an Alpha Course and completely changed. I remember getting back to my cell after a church service which I only attended because it got me out of my cell for a while and helped me manage the tedium. I remember saying

"God, I don't know if you exist but if you do, please help me build a relationship with my mum".

I didn't think anything would happen, I thought I was just throwing some words into the air. I put my head down for a sleep and when I awoke I felt different, calmer than I had felt in a long time. This was about a year or so into my sentence.

I got about completing my sentence and a few weeks later received a letter from my mum asking to visit. When she came she told me that I reminded her so much of my father but wanted me in her life. She wanted to quit the life but didn't know what else to do.

I told her that I had found God and was doing education. She decided that she wanted to go to night school and learn something new and perhaps get a job. We made a pact that day that she would leave the sex industry and I would work on getting out. She kept to her promise. She works with street girls trying to help them escape that life and I work as a support worker with the offenders and travelers within the prison system to help them build a better life.

....

Chapter Notes

I have known of Jake for almost as many years as I have been in Norfolk. In fact Jake was one of the first to obtain a personal signed copy of my first book. I knew a little of his story, mainly to do with his addiction and faith but I did not know his story to the extent that I do now.

Jake is one of those people I would gladly call a pal, more of an acquaintance to be honest. I met him when I first started to go to certain recovery meetings. He mainly kept to himself but would always find the time to ask me how I was doing. When I left I didn't see him for quite a while. When we did bump into each other on the street he would always find the time to stop and talk.

I hadn't seen him in a couple of years and he had heard I had written a book and proceeded to buy a digital copy. Upon our chance meeting he had found out that it was out in paperback and I gave him one there and then.

After reading the book he contacted me to congratulate me on the quality of the book. During the conversation I told him about my idea for this book and he was only too happy to help as long his anonymity was kept intact.

The Irish Rose

I suppose Ireland is a beautiful place in parts and it's alright to live if you are in the cities like Dublin, relaxed but a great nightlife and fun loving attitude, but like many places it has its dark parts.

I grew up in a small town just outside Limerick. Slow paced but alright for the craic I suppose. I love Ireland for that, the thing I don't love is some of the rules, especially the religious ones but I always kept my views to myself, especially having a deeply religious family. I never had a problem with church or faith but after I found myself pregnant at 17 after a drunken one night stand I found myself on the wrong side of the religious divide.

My parents were devastated and deeply offended I might add. Their daughter unmarried and pregnant, well what would the neighbours say. I was not ready to be a mother and in some ways I was still a child myself but the law in Ireland forbids abortion.

My father, who was more deeply religious than my mother refused to let me live under his roof anymore and told me I was moving in with an old spinster aunt's house who lived miles away from anywhere and I would be forced to live there and have the baby. I won't go too much into detail but there was a massive argument and I left home and contacted a cousin in England who agreed to let me live with her. So, as I left my father told me that if I was going to go to England I would never be allowed to come home. Both my mother and I were in tears, but I could not live the life they wanted. I had some money saved, enough for a one way ticket to London.

My cousin met me at the train station, I hadn't seen her since we were 7. She was beautiful and glamorous. She told me that I would have a home for as long as I needed. After I explained the full situation to her she offered to help me get an abortion and even pay for a private one. I told her that it was a lot of money to pay, she said that I was family and she could afford it.

She took me to her apartment and it was beautiful, she drove a sports car and wore the nicest clothes. I thought she must have a good job, a Solicitor or something. She gave me the reign of the apartment whilst she was out, I remember thinking that she worked odd hours, I told you I was naïve. She would bring back gifts from people she called clients.

I wasn't there long before she had booked the abortion for me at a private clinic. I won't go too far into it but I went through with the abortion, and yes I do regret it. Had I had the child it would be 17 now, the same age I was when my life changed. After my short recovery I wanted to find a job but I was struggling to find anything. I had no qualifications or experience. I told my cousin this and she said that she could get me work when I reached 18 in a couple of months time and until then she would take care of me.

I asked her what the job was and I was shocked when she told me she was an escort. I thought she meant she was some sort of carer for old people and she laughed when I said that. She explained that she would go on dates with lonely men, that they would pay for her company. That being an escort was as much about giving them company more than sex, although sex sometimes happens. "The girlfriend experience" she called it. She told everyone that it was always safe, with condoms.

I wasn't sure, I'd obviously had sex, several times, but with one boy in my town and we had known each other for years and the only time we did it without contraception I fell pregnant. The whole subject of contraception is a difficult one in Ireland, especially with Catholicism. Mind you sex before marriage is a no no too. Contraception and abortion are deeply frowned upon within the faith, especially abortion which by most, including my parents, is seen as murder. I had broken those rules of faith. I wasn't really what you can call a woman of faith anyway, a lapsed Catholic you might say. I only went to church because my family did, because I was made to, not because I wanted to. I didn't have to make the decision now anyway, my 18th birthday was a few months away.

I did think about it, a lot in fact. I tried to find a job and managed to find a part time waitressing job but that barely covered my expenses. By the time

92

I had reached 18 I had decided to give escorting a go. What did it matter anyway? It's only a date, it's only sex, I'd had it before, it was pleasurable to an extent and I could make some money and get by on my own. I wanted a good life. If anything I wanted to show my parents that I didn't need them, that I could be successful. I wanted the sports car, the Chelsea apartment, the fine clothes, the jewellery. I wanted my cousin's life, I wanted to be like her, so what the hell - I was going to do it, so I told my cousin yes.

A few nights later she would take me to meet her "manager" in the lobby of a very posh London hotel. As my cousin and I were roughly the same size she gave me one of her beautiful dresses to wear and jewellery. Now I should say that although I always looked feminine, long hair etc I was always the Tomboy. I would be in the fields chasing the lads with sticks. I would be the first to get dirty and the last to get clean. I didn't really know what is was like to be "Girly" so to be in a dress and high heels was a little out of my comfort zone.

We met an older lady by the name of Christine, a well to do woman in the lobby of the hotel and she took us into the bar. I won't go too much into the conversation but she said I had the potential to be a beautiful lady but I was "a little rough around the edges", that I needed some "Training". I must admit I had to stifle back a giggle because I pictured scenes from the film Pretty Woman. I have to say I wasn't wrong, I had very little etiquette.

I was told that my cousin and I would be picked up on Saturday morning and that I would be taken to buy appropriate clothing and be taken to a beauty salon for a makeover. This wasn't a gift she told me but as my manager she would take a small amount of "commission" for her help and a little off the top to pay back the loan in small payments but not to worry I would get to keep most of the money for myself. Call me naïve but it sounded fine to me.

My cousin would go through the points with me, you know…how to stand, how to walk, how to hold myself in public, Christine would go through the finer ones with me like how to eat, how to smile, what to say etc.

It started out with a few "Dates". These were mostly in the hotel lobby or a nearby restaurant. There would always be someone watching in case anything went wrong, they were never any less than 20 feet away, strategically positioned to get to me quickly if needed.

Of course I made a few errors to start with, the wrong fork or forgetting to smile or laugh in the right places.

I always had money, I was enjoying the life and when I was more confident, Christine told me that I was ready to offer the full girlfriend experience and I knew what that meant. To be honest I had really come to terms with the fact that I was going to have to have sex, but this meant more money and I could save to buy the apartment, the car, the life so I was strangely comfortable with it and I was ready. What I wasn't ready for was the pain of the full body waxing that would ensue.

The first time I offered a girlfriend experience was a nightmare, anything that could go wrong did. It was so awkward and uncomfortable. I couldn't wait to get it over with much to the dismay of my employers.

It began to get easier over time and I actually built a friendship with some of the regular clientele. It didn't take long before I had more money than I knew what to do with. I had the car, the apartment, the clothes, the makeup, the possessions, yet oddly I had begun to become unhappy. My mental health was becoming an issue and I wanted to stop. I had enough money to live well for a few years, so I decided that I wanted to take a break.

The thing about being an escort working for others is that time off and holidays are not something that you can demand, as I would soon find out.

I told Christine that I needed some time away, to get myself right in the head, to take care of me. I was thinking maybe 6 months to a year, after all I didn't really need the money anymore, I was making thousands of pounds a night. Christine told me that I could have a couple of weeks, but I had a good client base. I was making money for me but also for them. I told her I needed longer and she just went quiet and held a disapproving look upon her face.

My cousin and I went abroad for a couple of weeks. She hadn't really known I had gone to Christine, she just thought we were going on holiday. When I told her about the conversation she became concerned. I won't go into the details but she told me that Christine wouldn't let me go easily and that I should have spoken to her before going to Christine.

To say I was worried would be a vast understatement.

When I returned to my apartment there was the biggest bunch of roses I had ever seen waiting on the doorstep. There was a card that simply said "Get Well Soon....C".

I thought nothing of it really apart from it was a nice gesture. I had been home less than a day and the phone rang, it was of course Christine. She genuinely sounded concerned about my welfare and asked me how I was doing, if I had reconsidered taking a long break. When I told her no, she sounded disappointed but told me to take care of myself.

I guess it had been a couple of weeks and the phone calls started. 10 to 20 a day. It got so bad that I had to change my number. Every time I left the apartment I was being followed, it was so obvious it was unnerving.

My cousin had turned up on my doorstep, she had been threatened and told if she didn't get me back she would be harmed. I didn't know what to do, we couldn't go the police so I made arrangements to go and see her.

BIG MISTAKE! The biggest of my life!

Christine was nice at first when I met her at a bar. She told me that she did not want to let me leave but if I really wanted to then we could come to some arrangement. What could I do? I was scared for the safety of myself and my cousin, who by now had decided that she wanted to leave but was scared for her safety as well as mine.

All the time I had been under the assumption that I controlled my own life as a high class escort. For some reason I never made a distinction between street worker, brothel worker and escort. I guess it was a mix between snobbery and the lack of education or empathy. I could not really comprehend the difference between choosing a life in the sex industry and being forced. Of course I had heard of trafficking and sexual slavery but it was something that I ignored, through ignorance I guess. I think it comes down to perception. Rightly or wrongly, we do not see those things that are just out of sight. You know they are there, that they exist, but for some reason we choose not to see them. We do not acknowledge them because of our own reasons.

Whilst the sex Industry exists and where there is a constant call for sex workers (and I use that term widely) then people will be exploited. I never believed that I had been exploited until I tried to leave, it was only then that I saw these people for who they were. They were the puppet masters who care about nothing more than cold hard cash and they do not care who they exploit, who they tread on to get what they desire. These people controlled us by fear, by intimidation and cold hard threats. We knew that if we were to run we would never be able to look back and that it would be unlikely that we could ever return to the city, that we would always be looking over our shoulders.

When it came down to it, my cousin could not bring herself to leave but I did not want to go without her, she implored me to run and not look back. We worked out a system to keep in contact and I ran as fast and as far as I could.

I was told that I could leave but I would have to work until they could find a suitable girl to take over my regular clients and I would also have to buy myself out and they set an unreasonable buy out price of £20,000. I knew I had the money to come from the sale of my apartment and car and would have enough to get by for a little while after, but that would have me waiting for too long. I felt so down trodden and heartbroken, I just wanted to leave and that was apparent in the look on my face.

Christine was a very cold and calculating woman and as I found out, devious and brutal. She seemed to show concern for me, I now know that she was somewhat a chameleon when it came to facial expressions and could use them to her will, to her benefit.

She suggested that the easiest and quickest way would be to work a party, that there would be several men in one night. I have learned the hard way that there is never an easier or softer way to get what you want, we all pay for our decisions, our mistakes, however this was a price I was willing to

96

pay just to be free. I was used to working through several men in one day so how hard could this be.

I won't go into the details of the party but I will say that I was used and abused by over a half a dozen men at a time. They did unforgettable and depraved thing to me whilst she watched, smiling the whole time. I could barely walk when I was finally allowed to leave. I was told I could never tell anyone about them and if I did they would find me and kill me.

I didn't even go back to the apartment. I had emptied my primary bank account a few days before and put it in a locker at a train station and left instructions for my cousin in case I was not able to escape. I had made arrangements for the money for my apartment and car to go directly to my cousin and only she knew how to get it to me.
I left the country as fast as I could, I ran and never looked back. I will not tell you where I am, I will only tell you that I am happy.

When I spoke to the author of this book he called me a brave warrior, a beautiful survivor. I really wish I could feel like that but I cannot. I am not always strong, I get scared. I still look over my shoulder, I still have nightmares. I cry almost every day. I miss my family and although I regularly speak to my cousin I have not seen her in nearly 10 years. I have not seen or spoken to my actual family since the day I left and I miss them every day, but I do not have the courage to contact them for fear of being turned away.

I guess one of the lasting effects of the whole ordeal has lead to a fear of intimacy. I struggle to make lasting relationships with people in fear of them getting hurt. Not physically but emotionally, spiritually hurt when they find out about the life I led and the choices I have made. The damage has been done.

I'm not confident and I do not tell too many people my story. The only reason I speak out now is to try and educate people who are thinking that selling your body for cash is harmless, that sex is natural so what is the harm.

The trouble is that it is not just the body you sell, it is the soul.

…………..…………………………………………………..................................

Chapter Notes

I cannot comment too much on this testimony because of the promises I made to the contributor. It is my belief that all survivors (of any trauma not just exploitation) are beautiful courageous souls whether they believe it or not. I for one have made some monumentally stupid and downright dangerous decisions in my lifetime.

We all have our regrets, our skeletons in the cupboard (I often joke about having a full graveyard in mine). It is not how we deal with them at the time, it is how we deal with them now.

I am a great advocate in the belief that we cannot change our past but we should not wish to shut the door on it. Our mistakes have been made and we cannot change them only deal with the damage caused.

Some struggle with that chain of thought and it leads to self destructive behavior. It affects our lives, our relationships and our whole outlook upon life. This then leads us to pushing people away, often the ones we love the most.

What I will say is that no matter what the situation, no matter how much you want to give up, DON'T. Keep on fighting. Courage comes in many forms and speaking about your life in a book, anonymous or otherwise takes a great deal of courage.

Love, Honour and Obey

Sara

I made you a promise, before a congregation, before my family, my friends, standing before you and before God. I made you a promise to be the best wife I could be. To love you, to honour you with our union, two people now one unit before God. I promised to obey you, to be a good wife and I was proud to call you my husband. Our whole lives were parallel, I was the shy little geeky girl and you were the cool boy next door. We would play together on the street every day after school and every Saturday, only going in when we had to, usually when the streetlights went out. I was 9 and your were 10.

Remember?

I do, I also remember how protective you were if another kid upset me. You would hold me, pull me in tight and tell me everything will be ok, you will protect me and assure me its ok to cry.

I remember the first time you held my hand, firm yet it felt safe, I felt so protected with you. We were walking through the city centre on the way to the cinema on a Saturday morning. I held a smile upon my face, you always looked so serious but if you caught me gazing at you would give me a cheeky smile. You even let me choose the film, do you remember? it was Ghost, the matinee showing. You did not moan you just smiled and handed me the tissue when the tears fell as The righteous brothers played as Patrick sat behind Demi and they made a clay pot (among other things).

I remember your confusion near the end when they finally got to touch each other with the help of the medium and you proclaimed "So he is alive again then?" and then the confusion continued when I tried to explain how.

I remember ever single look, every single smile and almost every word you spoke to me. I was so in awe of you. How could a girl like me get a boy like you?

I remember our first kiss, I was shaking and you held me close, my knees went weak and I felt that kiss in the depths of my stomach that I did not know existed and I knew it was love.

I remember all those little things that made you, those little things that made us, even though we were still young.

I remember the first time we made love and you spent the whole time trying not to hurt me, being gentle and loving all whilst make me feel special, calling me your queen.

I remember your excitement when you got your first job, you told me you wanted to take care of me for the rest of our lives. I remember all those little things that made us, that made you, that made me fall deeper and deeper into love with you.

I would have done anything for you, and I did. I remember those things.

I remember when you asked me to marry you, your nervousness, as If I would have said anything but yes. I never had any doubts, I loved you with everything thing I had.

So there we were on our wedding day, trembling before the priest as we made our vows, our promises, meaning every word.

I remember these things so why did you forget so quickly? Is it because I became yours ?.

I remember that look like it was yesterday, you know the one when the man smiled at me in the airport on the way to our Honeymoon and I smiled back out of politeness. It was a look I had never seen before and you just went silent, your tone was unfamiliar when you finally did speak they were short and sharp spoken in a somber tone. The whole journey you forced a smile when you felt you needed to. I remember the way you held my hand on the aeroplane, firm as always, yet it felt different, if felt forced. I remember every drink you had, 6 in such a short time, but I said nothing because I had obviously upset you but didn't know how or why.

I remember that night, how could I ever forget? I went to put my hand on your face lovingly to assure you I didn't mean whatever I must of done but you slapped my hand away with such force my hand hit the wall and I cried out in pain, such pain that tears instantly fell from my eyes, and I know it was my fault because you told me in a roundabout way, taking the blame without actually taking the blame, I will never forget those words, yet again how could I?.

"I'm sorry you hurt your hand I should not have pushed it away but you shouldn't have done what you did, you shouldn't have put your hand to my face. I'm sorry you are hurt but you should really know not to flirt with other men.

And when I was confused and asked

"What men"?

I knew you were upset that I didn't know by your silence and your silence always speaks volumes. You just smiled, and later in bed when we made love, well it wasn't making love was it, it was just sex to you because I could see it behind your eyes you were just consummating our marriage, doing your legal duty.

you held that same smile, that smile I would come to know all too well, as you got rougher, no longer tactile, just animalistic as you got harder and harder till it began to hurt and the ecstasy that was every time before was quickly fading, no longer passion in my moans only pain in my screams and when I begged you to stop, when it hurt so much and my discomfort became a floodgate of tears you just smiled more as you covered my mouth.

You didn't stop, you just went harder, as hard as you could

I was no longer crying, I was screaming into your hand until you stopped, growing like a rabid dog and you just rolled off and walked away leaving me emotionally dying. It wasn't sex was it, let's call it what it is.

It was rape

But I was so blinded back then, I couldn't see what was going on right in front of my own eyes because I didn't know a husband could rape his wife, I thought it was the way it was, a mistake you would never repeat, perhaps in your blinded passion he didn't hear me say stop, you got Carried away, right.

But then it happened again

And again, and again so I stopped saying anything, learned to deal with the pain because that is what a good wife does isn't it? obeys her husband especially in the bedroom because that's his right, a husband can't rape his wife, I know, I remember what you said

"A husband controls the wife in the marital bed"

And if I resisted you would remind me with a "Gentle Reminder" a slap across the face to remind the good wife where her place is.

I remember you would remind me when I needed to look nice for you, dress nice, a little make up to look good good although too much and I look like a slut.

I remember how you would tell me if I ate too much, after all I wouldn't want to be fat, no husband wants a fat wife, right?

I lived for the days when you were in a good mood, when work went well and you only had enough alcohol in your system to make you placid. You would tell me how much you loved me. It would always end in sex, but times like this you would be gentle, I would see a little of the old you, the man I fell in love with, but these times were few and far between.

I remember you would remind me when I got thing wrong like the wrong word or saying, you would just laugh and call me stupid.

I remember you teaching me to have manners, how could I forget that sting, the reminder that a wife should be polite.

I remember the time you bought me those presents except they were not for me were they ?, the red lipstick and the sexy black laced underwear and stockings, you told me to model them for you only after a shower and I was clean and when I was clean enough and dressed I was to wait on the bed like the good queen and you would reward me with a treat, a surprise, only I had no choice, I was going to get it whether I wanted it or not, the word consent meant nothing to you, especially as you drugged my drink and how can I object if I am barely conscious. I remember the hazy limbo, unable to think, to move and you watched your friends one by one have their way. I could feel every sweaty, dirty touch as only God knows how many men abused my body as you just watched so husband how much is a soul of you wife worth ?, because those action suffocated mine into oblivion.

Part of me died that night as I resigned myself to a life in your sexual servitude, after all how could I lose you?, you had spent years drumming in the fact that I could not live without you, cope without you, after all who else would put up with the stupid fat wife, only you were brave enough or daft enough to take up that task and how grateful should I be and woe betide me if I didn't show my gratitude towards your generosity.

I remember your appetite, your lust as you sold me to your friends again and again and again and you no longer bothered to drug me, at least in that state I could hide behind the haze, and when they had finished you would call me a whore, yours to do with as you please, not just a whore, your whore on sale or return.

I remember every single look, every single word. The look you once gave me, you know the one, the one that brought me goosebumps, the one that made me weak at the knees now gone. The only thing that your stare brings in fear. The man I loved so much with every ounce of emotion now gone, the man who set me free became my jailer.

I remember when you would hit me, your own personal punch bag, you did it out of fun, no longer love here only you sadistic mind.

I remember you coming home drunk so I just fed you whatever alcohol we had until you went past violent and left me with a black eye. You went past the animal who wanted to fulfill his sexual needs and it was my pleasure because I knew you would pass out.

And you did pass out

I saw the door, I saw a way out, a new life and do you remember what I did?

....

Chapter Notes

I had almost finished the book, the main body of text was finished and I was just waiting for the forward and afterword to arrive, in fact the draft was already with my publisher Warcry Press when I was contacted by Sara's sister. To be honest I wasn't really looking for anymore content as the whole process of writing the book and transcribing some of the content had left me emotionally exhausted, I just wanted to take a day or two before I started planning the next book but something didn't feel right, this is a feeling every writer knows all too well, no matter how much they put in there is always a feeling that there needs to be more, however I agreed to speak anyway before I made the ultimate decision on whether to include it or not. From the very start of this project I made a promise to myself, to the survivor network and in faith to act as a voice for those who needed it but desired to maintain anonymity and also use this project to voice their stories and opinions. In my experience everyone has a story about something but don't always have the time or the skill set to do so. Don't get me wrong, each and every person I spoke to about this book have showed tremendous courage and integrity. They have all been difficult to listen and respond too and Sara's story is no different.

Sara is a softly spoken shy women which due to the circumstances I cannot say I am surprised about. For her trust, especially around men is a major issue.

As with all of the survivors in this book a plan of action was discussed. I wanted to make sure that every chapter projected their voice yet also make it individuality its content, a collaborative effort between myself and the survivor.

I was told by her sister that she had been given a copy of my first book to read as in her own words is "an avid bookworm". After reading it she passed it on to Sara to read. They began following my work and when they found out about this project they felt they should contact me.

I very much doubt that Sara lacks the skill set, the education or even the courage to write her own book, she like many lacks the confidence to do so at the moment. She felt she had so much to say but didn't know or understand how to communicate it due to the PTSD she suffered wasn't able to commit to anything so bold and as many of my readers know PTSD is very relevant in my own life only one of the ways I manage my own is by using creativity and working on projects like this.

Sara professed to being a fan of my first book (a personal apocalypse) and loved the way I structured many of the chapters. For Sara this whole exercise was an attempt to not only to try to improve her mental health but I have a feeling she needed to find a cathartic means to let go of certain parts of her past.

She wanted the chapter to not only read like a letter but also be a way of letting out events, making her point clear (which she did well) whilst having the poetic tone of my previous work, this took some time to organise and work on, as with every other story in this book I wanted a unique mix of all of our voices. One thing I did not wish to do was put words into any of the survivor's mouths nor did I wish to ultimately influence the outcome of the chapters. The survivors come first, their needs and what they want, what I wanted was always on the back burner.

When Sara read the result of the interviews and my work she told me that it was like I was able to speak from her mind, she told me that it is exactly what she wanted to say with nothing missing, she just felt she was not able to communicate as effectively as myself and that seeing it written, although slightly triggering was now a pivotal part of her Recovery.

Sara, you know who you are, I hope and pray that along with the other survivors that this book not only projects your collective voice, tells your unique story, shows your tremendous courage, educates those that need it and ultimately helps toward becoming stronger and become the Warriors you are meant to be.

I Ran

As fast, as far as I could and I never looked back.

In the beginning You were my love, my all, my reason to live and in the end you were nothing but the reason I wanted to die, and I tried, more than once but now I know that had I succeeded you would have won and believe me you nearly did.

I remember being a victim, weak and feeble. I remember being so reliant on you after all you told me how to live. I wasn't a woman to you, I don't even think you saw me as human but you certainly saw me as the victim, the weak and feeble woman at home, your play toy and punch bag.

I remember when it happened, when I changed, when I transitioned from victim to survivor. I simply let you go no longer to live rent free in my head. No longer my captor, my jailer, my life.

I became a butterfly from the cocoon you had me trapped inside. My fight, my will, my instincts had laid dormant for so long and now I am ready for flight. I am no longer your slave, your captive.

I survived and I am free

Finally

Sincerely
Me

The Lost

Growing up I never really had a positive image of myself. I was the fat kid, teased and bullied because of his size, because he was different to the apparent norm. This negative attitude was normalised at home with so called banter and in the name of fun and love. Little digs at my ego and Nicknamed Tiny by my father in the name of irony. By the time I had reached 15 I was 6 feet 5 inches tall and almost 18 stone. I had decided somewhere around the age of 13 that the bullying would never stop unless I did something's about it myself and I got into fitness, weightlifting and boxing so as I said at 15 I was near enough pure muscle.

I would still get the looks when I was out, people would turn around and mutter about my size, I didn't ignore it, I didn't even react I would just walk on by with a smile and the pain hidden deep inside to be used as fuel when I fought in the ring or when I needed to get those extra reps in before muscle failure at the end of a work out. I worked personal security for a while, worked on the doors of dive nightclubs. I had no ties in the UK, I had stopped talking to my family several years before, I had some savings so I decided I was going to look into moving to the USA. I had decided that an stopover in Amsterdam was on the cards and as it happened the moment I stepped into the city I fell totally in love with the place, not for the Drugs, Not for the prostitution but for its relaxed attitude and the stunning beauty of the pink blossoms that line the river, the friendly local attitude, however at the time the Cannabis and women were a bonus.

Prostitution in the Netherlands had been legal for a few years before I arrived. To be honest there were a few street workers but it was mostly legal brothels around the country, however the Amsterdam Red-light district is the most famous and aesthetically pleasing to a certain type of person. Women displayed in Windows in the most alluring way and the men they shop with little or no thought and choose women like they would a meal deal from the local petrol station.

This was a time when some of the brothels of the city could have been tied to organised crime, (not all I must add, I should also say I left years ago and not really in the know about how it may be these days, one could presume that the same applies, However I cannot be sure). This was mostly down to the odd eastern European and Jamaican syndicates. These were the highest turnover and usually used as a front for the more sinister dealings. I have met a great many sex workers in one form or another and I have heard stories of human trafficking.

There is only so much of that lifestyle a man can take before he begins to question his morality, and I am no different. I had become tired of living in Amsterdam and as a result I took a lot of personal security work outside of the city.

I was on my way back to the UK to see some friends and heading towards the hook of Holland to catch a ferry back to England. I stopped off at a nearby bar for refreshments and was sitting outside in the beer garden enjoying a smoke and a pint when I was approached by a young Irish girl, no older that 22 I guess. She explained that she was working her way to Amsterdam to find work in the sex industry. She had no money, very few clothes and wondered if I was interested in having sex with her so she could at least earn some food or perhaps a cheap room for the night. She looked so innocent and there was no way that I would have taken advantage of her. Yes during my time there I had experienced the company of the odd sex worker and it never bothered me, but something felt different about this girl. I respectfully declined but I bought her a meal, paid for a room in a nearby B&B and gave her a few quid to get by. After I had sorted her out I was going to leave, in fact I was about to go into the ferry terminal but something didn't feel right. I had this voice in my head telling me to go back to her, she needed my help.

I had never been religious in my life, I didn't believe for one minute it was or would ever be a supernatural experience, I just put it down to my own thoughts, perhaps I was being silly. I wanted to go to the terminal but I was frozen on the spot, I couldn't move a muscle. "I just wanna get my ferry" I told myself but my mind kept saying "Go back, she needs you". I still couldn't move and that voice in my head was unfamiliar. I thought I was going mental, hearing voices that were not my own. Yet as soon as I made the decision to turn back I could move again. I didn't know whether it was my own mind, Guilt or God that held me there until I submitted to the fact I was going to look for her.

I went back to the B&B I had paid for and went to her room and knocked on the door but there was no answer yet I had the strangest feeling she was in there. The odd strange gurgling sound coming from the room. I ran down to the reception and by showing my receipt I got a spare key. When I got into the room there she was naked on the bathroom floor, needle hanging out of her arm, she had overdosed on heroin. I managed to get her to the hospital and sat with her until she came around.

We spoke for hours and I'd like to think I made a difference, truth is that I may never know as I left the Netherlands that week after I had managed to secure her a place in a rehabilitation program. I never saw or heard from her again. The optimist in me hopes she is alive and well however I know the grip that drugs can have on people.

Not long after I returned to the UK I changed my job and retrained to become a support worker. I work mainly with street workers looking for a fresh start. There are some who have made great lives for themselves outside of the sex industry, yet there are still many who need the right help, however whilst there is a need for sexual services there will always be a need for sex workers hence exploitation in one form or another, so something needs to change.

....

Chapter Notes

Stephen was kind enough to contact me after finding out about my project. He wanted to get across the point that no matter who you are or what you have done in your life there is always room for change and ways of doing that.

For some there is no foreseeable way out of sex work and sexual exploitation. Were it not for people like him I am sure that more people would be trapped in that vicious cycle.

Thank you for your service Stephen you are appreciated my friend.

Final Thoughts

I have spoken to so many people over the past 6 months or so and I have been affected by every single story I have been told. These survivors are amongst the strongest people I know and each and every one is a warrior whether they believe it or not.

There are so many people who are still trapped in that vicious cycle, trapped in the abuse and have not yet managed to find the strength to stand up.

When I began this book my goal was only to help convey stories in hope that they may affect and educate people into wanting to make a change. We live in a world where there is so much injustice and something needs to be done.

For me writing this book, helping convey these stories, giving a voice to the survivors and in certain situations becoming the voice of the survivors has changed me inside out and for that I am truly blessed and grateful for the opportunity to be a part of the education and information process.

Thank you to everyone who has bought this book and managed to read to the end, I fully understand how difficult it may have been, there were times when I thought I may not be able to finish. There are times the emotion got to me a lot.

Thank you for your continued support

Jack

Spotting The Signs And Symptoms Of Possible Abuse

These lists are far from exhaustive and signs can often be obvious or subtly hidden. The signs are there, we just need to learn how to spot them and deal with them appropriately. I would not be doing my duty as an Activist and Writer of a book that tackles the subjects of trafficking and exploitation if I neglected a chapter like this. To not do so would be neglectful.

Looking at the subject of abuse, especially in children, your first thought may be of children with marks and bruises that may raise a Red Flag. However the truth is that the signs may not always be clear. Signs and symptoms can often be physical, sexual and emotional.
They may be neglected, this means the care giving adults may well not provide for basic life needs such as food or personal safety.

Abuse is hard to stop and what makes it more difficult to stop is that more often than not, the abuser can be someone the child knows, this may often be a family member or someone in a position of trust or even loved. The child may well be reluctant to speak out because they want to protect the abuser from getting into trouble for fear of what they may do if caught.

It is so important that as adults we are able to distinguish the signs and symptoms, the different types of abuse and what we should do if we suspect it.

Types of child abuse

Abuse in children happens when someone harms the child's body, development, emotional health and wellbeing.

The 4 Types of abuse;

Physical abuse

Physical abuse means that a child's body may be hurt or being put into physical danger. It makes no difference if the child gets seriously hurt or if a mark is left. ANY HARM WHATSOEVER is abuse.

This includes:

- Hitting
- Kicking or biting a child
- Shaking or throwing the child
- Burning a child
- Bonding or binding the child in any way
- Throwing things at the child

Sexual abuse

Sexual abuse is any kind of sexual activity with a child and not is limited to just physical contact.

This includes:

Any form of sexual contact including kissing in a sexual way and any form of sexual contact.

Forcing the child to pose for inappropriate pictures, take part in inappropriate videos:

- The showing of Pornography
- The showing of genitals for instance flashing
- Telling dirty and inappropriate jokes or stories.
- Making 'phone calls, sending texts or emails, direct messages through apps like Facebook, Twitter, Instagram etc and sending inappropriate pictures via these methods.

Emotional abuse

Emotional abuse is certain patterns of behaviors that will harm a child's well being and emotional development. This can mean when somebody:

- Threatens
- Teases
- Shouts
- Bullies
- Fails to be affectionate and show love
- Ignoring the child and not giving them the guidance and emotional support that is needed.
- Shames
- Belittles
- Criticises
- Calls them names.

Neglect

Neglect is when the caregiver will not give the child the basic protection and care that they need, such as:

- Heat in cold weather
- Basic medical care
- Basic dental care
- Clean housing with more than basic living conditions
- Clothing
- Food

Neglect is also when a caregiver leaves the child alone for extended lengths of time or under dangerous conditions.

Abuse is often hard to recognise. Kids being kids often end up covered in marks and bruises. Children can also manifest the symptoms of stress for many reasons, this is a perfectly normal part of childhood.

It helps to know the specific signs to look for. Follow your instincts and trust them as you look at the bigger picture of the child's emotional and physical health.

Signs of physical abuse might include:

- Untreated medical and dental issues
- Burns, especially those of cigarettes that cannot be explained
- Injuries at different stages of healing

Injury marks that may have a pattern such as hand, belt, shoe etc.
Welts, bruises, marks or other injuries that cannot be explained or does not match the child's story.

Children whom are being physically abused may also:

- Be fearful of going home
- Avoid any form of contact or physical touch
- Be withdrawn from normal activities and friendships
- Wear clothing that may not match the weather, i.e. long sleeves on a hot day to hide bruises and marks.

Signs of sexual abuse can include:

- Avoiding people for no clear reason
- Torn, bloody or stained underwear
- Bleeding, bruising and marks around the genital area
- Itching or pain around the genital area that could cause problems sitting or walking.

- STD's or Pregnancy, this is especially prevalent in children under 14 years old.
- Constantly running away from home or school.
- Refusing to change clothing in front of others.
- Sexual activity and/or knowledge that surpasses their age knowledge.

Signs of emotional abuse:
- Depression
- Low self esteem
- Constantly worrying

- Achieving lower than their normal grades in school
- Unexplained headaches or stomach aches
- Delays in learning or speech problems in emotional development.
- Extreme behaviour, such as being way too demanding or way too obedient.
- Showing little or no interest in activities or normal friendships.

Signs of neglect:

- Always dirty, unkempt
- Being left alone to care for younger siblings
- Saving, stashing food, eating more than normal.
- Poor medical, dental care
- Poor weight and growth
- Missing school a lot.

So what can we do if we suspect abuse, needless to say that it is more than important to report it. Abuse in any form isn't a private matter or a family problem, it is a child's physical, mental, emotional and well being at stake. It may be even be their lives.

Proof is not needed to report child abuse. If you suspect it call the police, the hospital, social services or a hotline. You don't have to give your name if you are worried about repercussions.

If medical care is needed urgently call 999.
If you can take them to a hospital do so, a hospital is a safe haven for children. Doctors can look for signs and symptoms of abuse and give medical care.

If you think it may be someone like a baby sitter, a childminder, a playgroup worker or teacher who has abused your child, keep them away from that person and call the police immediately.

Help get them therapy, this will aid the journey to recovery from the abuse.

Make sure the child knows that it is not their fault, under no circumstances are they to blame.

And finally, although you may want to, and it would be tempting to, do not confront the abuser yourself. Call the police and let them deal with it. The child needs support, not to see someone they care about in jail or worse.

Recognising The Signs Of Human Trafficking And Sexual Exploitation

There is a world out there beside us. It parallels our lives yet we are often too rushed, too busy to see it. We know it is there yet often we choose not to see, to ignore it. That world just out of sight, just away from the corner of our eyes, seen but not seen. We are blinded by ignorance, by fear, by misunderstanding. It's not always our own faults, we are conditioned not to look. Those homeless in the doorway we turn away so we do not see. The big issue sellers we hide our change from, muffle the pocket change and don't make eye contact.

Those girls, yes THOSE girls in that promiscuous clothing waiting to tap a punter or two for a good time. Those girls who work the streets and brothels blended in the shadows to sell their sex. They want it, they love it, otherwise why on earth would they prowl the night?
Most of these girls have no choice, they are victims of their circumstances. Who else is going to look after them apart from the pimps and pushers.

Sexual exploitation and human trafficking need to stop. These girls rarely have a voice of their own which is why we need to step in and help. We need to know the signs of trafficking and exploitation so we can help them escape.

It is our duty to care. We need to know and recognize the Red Flags and know the indicators of trafficking and exploitation. These are not just girls on the street, ladies of the night. They are mothers, daughters, sisters, friends. This could happen to anyone, including you.

Common work and living conditions

Are they free to come and go as they please?

Are they under 18 and are to your belief providing commercial sex acts?

Are they in the commercial sex industry and has a pimp or "manager"?

Are they paid very little, not paid at all or only through commission or tips?

Do they work excessively long hours or unusual hours.

Are they not allowed breaks or do they suffer unusual conditions at work?

Do they owe a large debt that they are unable to pay?

Were they recruited through false promises concerning the nature of their work?

Poor mental health or abnormal behavior
Are they:

- Fearful
- Anxious
- Depressed
- Submissive
- Tense
- Nervous
- Paranoid

Do they avoid eye contact ?

Do they exhibit unusual anxious behaviour after bring up subjects like the police?

Do they seem to have poor physical health like:

- Lacking health care
- Appearing malnourished
- Show signs of physical abuse, sexual abuse
- Show signs of physical restraints or torture.

Lack of control

Has very few or no personal possessions.

Not in control of their own money, no financial records or bank account.

Not in control of their own documentation such as passport or ID card.

Are they allowed to speak for themselves or does someone else insist on speaking on their behalf / translating or being present?

Other

Do they claim they are just visiting and cannot clarify where they are residing?

Do they have a lack of knowledge of their whereabouts and may not know what city they are in?

Do they have a disjointed sense of time?

Do they have inconsistent stories?

Spotting if a child may be being trafficked or exploited.

The last list tackled adults but what about seeing the signs in children. These can me more difficult to spot and recognize. These may most likely be less obvious, you may however more commonly notice unusual or odd behavior and/or events.

These include a child who:

- Spends a lot of time doing household jobs
- Rarely leaves the house, has no noticeable freedom of movement, perhaps not time for playing
- Is orphaned or living away from their close family, often in unregulated foster care

- Lives in sustained accommodation
- Are not sure what city or town they may be in
- Unable or extremely reluctant to give personal details or speak about their accommodation
- May not be registered with medical professionals or school
- Has no documents or falsified documents
- Has no access to their parents or guardians
- Is seen in inappropriate places such as suspected brothels or factories
- Possesses unaccounted for money or goods
- Is permanently deprived of a large part of earnings, required to earn a minimum amount of money every day to pay off exorbitant debt
- Has injuries from workplace
- Gives a prepared story which is very similar to stories given by other children.

Signs and adult maybe involved in trafficking children

As well as learning to notice the signs in adults and children as in the previous chapter, to protect the vulnerable, we should also need to know how to recognize if an adult is involved with the trafficking of children and vulnerable adults. Here are just a few warning signs:

They are making or have made multiple visa applications for children and other people.

They are acting as a guarantor for multiple visa applications for other people and children.

They are seen traveling with different children they are not responsible for or even related to.

Insist on remaining with and/or insist on speaking on behalf of the person or child.

Living with unrelated or newly arrived children.

Abandoning a child or not claiming to know a child they were previously with.

Helplines

If you are in immediate danger always call the police, and always dial 999 if it is an emergency. They have a duty to protect and help you.

Crimestoppers

To report a crime anonymously, call: 0800 555 111

crimestoppers-uk.org

STOP THE TRAFFIC

Telephone: 020 7921 4258

E-mail: info@stopthetraffik.orgwww.stopthetraffik.org

Stop the Traffik is a global coalition working together to help stop the sale of people We believe that when people act, things change.

Our aim is to equip you to raise the awareness and understanding of human trafficking, and to make a difference and join the fight to STOP THE TRAFFIK.

English Collective of Prostitutes

Tel: 020-7482 2496

Crossroads Women's Centre
230a Kentish Town Road
London NW5 2AB

or

PO Box 287
London NW6 5QU

prostitutescollective.net

Since 1975, the International Prostitutes Collective has been campaigning for the abolition of the prostitution laws which criminalize sex workers and our families, and for economic alternatives and higher benefits and wages.

The RA Trust

National Sexual Health Helpline 0300 123 7123

ratrust.org.uk

Sex workers

The RA Trust is a charity dedicated to helping women and men involved in the sex industry. We are non-judgmental and support those working on the streets and in brothels.

Our aim is to help people who experience physical violence, rape, sexual abuse, torture, discrimination and other issues that can result in long-term physical and mental health illness. In the six years that we have been operating we have met almost 5,000 sex workers in different situations. We have been successful in helping 51 women leave the world of prostitution and they are now living lives they had only dreamed of.

At present we provide an outreach service for people working in the London boroughs of Redbridge and Newham but if you would like to meet us, we can travel to you. We provide sex workers with brochures and advice and, if they are ready, we can help them leave the sex industry. It is very important for us to keep them safe from HIV and sexually transmitted infections, which is why we give away hundreds of thousands of condoms every year.

Swish

swishproject.org.uk

Contact Swish

SWISH is a charity project which supports anyone involved in the sex industry. Our services are completely free and confidential, and we provide clinics, support work, outreach and counselling services. We are part of Terrence Higgins Trust and we support women, men and trans people who work in the adult industries. Whether you are a new flat-based sex worker or an experienced porn actor, we can help you with a broad range of issues - from practical matters, to support with emotional challenges. Whether you would just like to meet us for a one-off chat or whether you would like to work with us to create a plan tailored specifically to your needs, we're here to help.

UK Network of Sex Work Projects

uknswp.org

Resources

Member organisations are diverse and include:

Those that are located and managed within the national health service, local authority projects, third sector/voluntary organisations, sex worker led organisations and agencies with a faith based ethos and or/harm reduction and human rights.

Some member organisations have sexual health and HIV prevention as a major focus for their work, others have a drugs, sex worker rights, or wider health remit. Protection from violence, promoting safety, housing support, education, alternative lifestyle choices, exiting and the sexual exploitation of young people are also addressed.

Member organisations may be projects specifically for sex workers, or may address sex work issues within other agendas, such as youth work, drugs, sexual health, health promotion, or work with gay lesbian, bisexual and transgender people.

Individual members include academics and others with expertise in the area of sex work.

The Women's Library

Good resource with links to local help and support for sex workers.

Freedom Charity

Need Help Now: 0845 607 0133 (24 hours)

Textline: text '4freedom' to 88802

freedomcharity.org.uk

We aim to empower young people to feel they have the tools and confidence to support each other and have practical ways in which they can help their best friend around the issues of family relationships which can lead to early and forced marriage and dishonour based violence.

The Sophie Hayes Foundation

sophiehayesfoundation.org

Sophie Hayes Foundation on Facebook

Our mission is to raise awareness about, and support survivors of, human trafficking and modern day slavery.

The Sophie Hayes Foundation will support activities raising human trafficking awareness across social, business, governmental and political communities in order to challenge stereotypes, stimulate improved societal response, promote businesses to take responsibility, and ensure human trafficking and modern day slavery remain high on the political agenda, as well as supporting survivors of human trafficking and modern day slavery through career coaching and practical training for future sustainable employment free of Human Trafficking and Exploitation, and by working closely with other institutions and NGO's on similar projects.

Women's Aid 24hr Domestic Violence Helpline (run in partnership between Refuge and Women's Aid)

Freephone: 0808 2000 247 (24 hours)

nationaldomesticviolencehelpline.org.uk

The Helpline can give support, help and information over the telephone, wherever the caller might be in the country.

The Helpline is staffed 24 hours a day by fully trained female helpline support workers and volunteers. All calls are completely confidential. Translation facilities for callers whose first language is not English, and a service for callers who are deaf or hard of hearing are available.

Southall Black Sisters

Helpline: 0208 571 0800

southallblacksisters.org.uk

If you or someone you know is experiencing domestic violence, Southall Black Sisters can help with practical help and advice.

Our holistic service aims to help women and children escape violence and abuse (including forced marriage and honour crimes) and deal with a range of inter related problems.

Southall Black Sisters is a not-for-profit organisation set up in 1979 to meet the needs of black (Asian and African-Caribbean) and minority ethnic women. For more than three decades we have been at the forefront of challenging domestic and gender violence locally and nationally.

Honour Network - Karma Nirvana

Helpline: 0800 599 9247

karmanirvana.org.uk

Karma Nirvana is a registered Charity that supports victims and survivors of forced marriage and honour based abuse. We are your listening ear in confidence and many of us have the experience of forced marriage and issues related to honour based abuse. We are here for you when you're at home or when you leave and will talk over the phone wherever you are. One of our key principles is that we never talk to or engage with your family. Our commitment and loyalty is to you and as we understand the fears when family members become involved.Fm